Advance praise for *Reinventing Sunday*

Reinventing Sunday is a wonderful book! I came away from reading it refreshed, stretched, and challenged to be a more alive participant on the creative and recreative journey of authentic worship. The book is biblically grounded, theologically astute, experientially informed, and practically focused. It is a treasure chest of creative ideas, stimulating images, striking metaphors, and memorable quotes. Worship leaders and worshipers who allow the author to show them the way toward transformed and transforming worship will be delightfully rewarded! I thank God for this gift to the church from the heart and mind of Brad Berglund.

Manfred T. Brauch, Professor of Biblical Theology
Eastern Baptist Theological Seminary
Wynnewood, Pennsylvania

Brad Berglund is the kind of worship leader a pastoral team dreams of—ministering to heart, soul, mind, and strength through his gifts for music, drama, silence, and the spoken word. In this generously offered book, the author makes an accessible symphony of worship ideas, tips, counsel, and even sample services. Brad is a thoughtful and powerful worship leader who has always had the courage to integrate the truths learned living gloriously a painful human life. Because his is true worship, it is worship adaptable to a refreshing variety of settings. *Reinventing Sunday* is an eminently practical work. I left it energized to plan worship in new ways, and did.

Carol Holtz-Martin, Senior Pastor, Macedon, New York
American Baptist Churches USA

Worship leaders and planners will be enriched by *Reinventing Sunday,* which contains numerous breakthrough ideas for transforming worship. More important, it provides a base from which leaders can mold and shape a creative path appropriate to the worship challenges of their congregation. Brad Berglund's creative spirit permeates this book, as does his life experience.

Jan Chartier, Ph.D., Pastor and Former Seminary Professor
American Baptist Churches USA

This book is a gift! My spirit was nourished and blessed as I savored every page. Over and over again I wondered as I read if worship might not come alive in many of our own churches if pastors and worship leaders would study this book and take it to heart. Brad Berglund's experience, wisdom, and quiet passion shine forth in all he has written. If his creative suggestions alone were taken seriously, worship could be profoundly changed.

Roger Fredrikson, Pastor Emeritus
American Baptist Churches USA

Hear what the Spirit is saying through this one who speaks the truth about what it means to be an authentic worshiping community of believers. In *Reinventing Sunday*, Brad Berglund offers us the gift of himself as he shares a portion of his own liturgical journey for the benefit of all who design and implement worship. This is not a "formula for success" but rather vital and vibrant proof of the power of well planned and innovative worship to transform the life of a congregation.

Linda Bonn, Office of the General Secretary
American Baptist Churches USA
Author of The Work of the Worship Committee

This book is a passionate plea for the revisioning of worship and a challenging reflection on its meaning. New and ancient methods are presented for leading us out of ordinary time into God's own time where God is revealed and real. Evocative and heartwarming, this pastor gives us the gift of himself in his writing.

Sally Brower, Ph.D., Pastor, Christ Lutheran Church
Charlotte, North Carolina

This presentation of ideas for liturgical worship is a treasure trove of creative approaches for the age-old practice of Christian gathering. Not only the "whats" but the "whys" are spelled out. A must read for all liturgists. What a joyful place the church would be if these ideas were attempted.

R. A. Liddell, Sister of Loretto, Director
Thomas Merton Center, Denver, Colorado

Reinventing Sunday

Breakthrough Ideas for Transforming Worship

Brad Berglund

Judson Press
Valley Forge

Reinventing Sunday: Breakthrough Ideas for Transforming Worship
© 2001 by Judson Press, Valley Forge, PA 19482-0851
All rights reserved.

Bible quotations in this volume are from the following versions:
The New English Bible. Copyright © The Delegates of the Oxford University Press and The Syndics of the Cambridge University Press 1961, 1970. (NEB)
The New Revised Standard Version of the Bible, copyright © 1989 by the Division of Christian Education of the National Council of the Churches of Christ in the United States of America. Used by permission. All rights reserved. (NRSV)
THE MESSAGE. Copyright © 1993, 1994, 1995. Used by permission of NavPress Publishing Group.

Library of Congress Cataloging-in-Publication Data
Berglund, Brad.
Reinventing Sunday : breakthrough ideas for transforming
worship / Brad Berglund.
    p. cm.
Includes bibliographical references.
 ISBN 0-8170-1414-4 (pbk. : alk. paper)
 1. Public worship. I. Title.
BV15 .B45 2001
 264--dc21   2001029794

Printed in the U.S.A.
07 06 05 04 03 02
10 9 8 7 6 5 4 3 2

With gratitude to the congregations I've served:
First Baptist Church, Fresno, California
First Baptist Church, San Diego, California
Calvary Baptist Church, Denver, Colorado
because ordination gives a title
but people make a pastor

About the Author

Rev. Brad Berglund has been a pastor, church musician, and worship leader for twenty years.

His love for church music and worship began when he was a boy growing up in his father's church and singing in the youth choir. For more than a decade, Brad served as one of the pastors at Calvary Baptist Church in Denver, Colorado, where his responsibilities included worship creation and leadership, ministries of spiritual growth and creative expression, choral conducting, and leading an association of churches worshiping in the style of the Taizé community. In addition to earning degrees in classical guitar (studying with Doug Niedt at the conservatory of music at University of Missouri, Kansas City) and theology (Eastern Baptist Theological Seminary), he has completed the program for spiritual direction at the Shalem Institute in Washington, D.C. Brad has written many articles in the area of worship renewal and currently directs an ecumenical ministry called Illuminated Journeys, which offers sacred travel opportunities, spiritual renewal weekends, worship consulting, and Taizé-style workshops working with church musicians, pastors, and worship committees around the country.

Interested in Worship Renewal for your church or retreat?
Contact the author:
Brad Berglund
Illuminated Journeys
8273 E. Davies Avenue, Englewood, CO 80112
Phone: 720-489-8073
Toll Free: 877-489-8500
E-mail: brad@illuminatedjourneys.com
Website: www.reinventingsunday.com

Contents

ix **Foreword**
xi **Preface**
xiv **Acknowledgments**
xv **Introduction**

1 *The Prelude*
  3 **Chapter 1**   Understanding Worship
  12 **Chapter 2**   Starting on Purpose:
                      The Lost Art of Preparation

21 *Movement One: Gathering*
  23 **Chapter 3**   Gathering and Greeting
  28 **Chapter 4**   Praising and Singing
  38 **Chapter 5**   Praying

45 *Movement Two: Encountering*
  47 **Chapter 6**   Reading
  54 **Chapter 7**   The Preaching Moment

61 *Movement Three: Responding*
  63 **Chapter 8**   Communion
  67 **Chapter 9**   Giving
  73 **Chapter 10**   Baptism

77 *Movement Four: Embracing*
  78 **Chapter 11**   Sending

82 **Chapter 12**   Benediction and Response

87 The Postlude
88 **Chapter 13**   The Modulating Congregation
95 **Chapter 14**   Cleaning Up: Frequently Asked Questions

101 **Appendix A**   The Gift of Liturgical Time
106 **Appendix B**   A Home Dedication Service
111 **Appendix C**   A Healing Prayer Service
116 **Appendix D**   Worship and Prayer in the Style of the
                       Taizé Community

121 **Bibliography**

Foreword

FOR TWENTY-EIGHT YEARS, FIFTY SUNDAYS A year, I have found myself worshiping in somebody's church. I am usually asked to sing a considerable part of the service. Often I find myself in a situation where I am bored, the people are bored, the leaders are bored, and as the song from Westside Story suggests, "today the hours go so slowly, the minutes seem like hours."

But, once in a while I arrive in a place where it is quite clear that everyone involved is having an utterly wonderful time. People do not seem to want to leave; excitement is in the air; folks are wrestling with their lives; praise flows freely, and there is everywhere the evidence that these are today people romancing a today God with hearts full of gratitude.

In those places where I have found worship to be alive, whether the worship style is traditional or postmodern, whether the architecture is gothic or garage, whether the preaching comes from professor or plumber, this is the inescapable reality of that cosmic drama wherein we give ourselves away to God's promises: In that drama, by means ordinary and miraculous, predictable and surprising, natural and supernatural, our lives are changed.

If I were going to sum up what I have learned in church about worship through both negative and positive experiences, that summary would bear remarkable resemblance to this amazing book. Brad Berglund has captured what I believe is the rock-bottom essence of worship: namely, that it is offering ourselves to God. Berglund has structured his writing to make sense to a diverse group of worshiping churches, and his creative ideas flow as naturally from his premises as water from an artesian well.

This book will help worship leaders and worshipers in general to develop a theological and philosophical underpinning for their thinking about the crucial activity of worship. For those church communities that are lost in tradition that has become lifeless or that are dashing after the new until it has become tedious, this book bespeaks notions of balance and meaning. Most of all, it encourages those who lead to invite those who worship to do the work of worship.

The author encourages creativity but makes it clear that such creativity grows out of and facilitates congregational life. You will find in this book enough thoughtful reflection, enough creative ideas, and enough passion for God to refresh you along what can sometimes be a desert way.

William Stringfellow writes of his embarrassment when taking a friend to church only to sit through a wretchedly boring service. When church was over, Stringfellow apologized profusely to his friend, who reportedly replied something like, "Don't worry, at least now I know what church is not supposed to be." I suspect that diving into these pages will help us all imagine what church is supposed to be.

Ken Medema
Grandville, Michigan
Lent 2001

Preface

AS I SIT IN A HERMITAGE PERCHED ON A SAGE-covered plateau between the Sangre de Cristo Mountains and the San Luis valley in Southern Colorado, it's amazing to think that this entire area used to be under water. That's right—the visitor's center at the Sand Dunes National Monument says so. This was all an ocean. They have the fossils to prove it.

Churches have fossils, too. Okay, they're not millions of years old, but, nevertheless, they are hardened into place. People become fossilized. Church structures become rigid. Even worship—that weekly, sacred interaction with God—becomes fixed. It's understandable.

All organizations create zones of identity. When we find what works for the most people, we create patterns of behavior within those zones and give ourselves a name. With that label comes the need for consistency to meet established expectations and, voilà, we have a safe product created to avoid disappointing anyone familiar with our identity. Having a safe identity is comforting, but, by definition, it will keep us small. As the saying goes, "A ship in the harbor is safe, but that's not what ships are built for."

Close to my house is a wonderful fish and reptile shop. My son is a self-proclaimed shark expert so he enjoys going there to watch the sharks circle the tank. Through our frequent visits, I've learned a fascinating fact about these mysterious creatures. Sharks actually grow in proportion to the size of their tank. Put a shark in a small tank, and it grows to fit that tank size and then stops. Place the shark in a large aquarium and it grows to fit that environment. But put the shark in the vast expanse of the ocean, and the shark grows to the size it was created to be.

People, and the organizations they create, are like sharks. They grow in proportion to their environment. Churches are especially vulnerable to this growth-stunting phenomenon. Because Christians are free to associate with the church of their choice, they often become involved in a comfortable, like-minded environment. The tank size is established by free association. Restlessness within the ranks is often labeled as subversive; the troublemakers who are unconsciously shunned leave, and the aquarium stays intact.

Because the Holy Spirit cannot be controlled, spirited worship is spontaneous and thus a point of vulnerability for a religious institution. By definition, opening our lives to God in worship has an uncontrollable quality to it. In this environment of openness to divine leading, where God speaks and we respond, the church groans to become all it was meant to be. The word religion from the Latin *religio* means to re-attach. As the highest religious act, worship is a place of spontaneous re-attachment for people and their God.

Shaking off some of the fossilized debris from our worship designs may be the most direct way for a church to reconnect with God, to experience new life and be refreshed by an unexpected breath of the Spirit. This takes courage on the part of all involved. The risk is not to be taken lightly. Many of us do not want to expand in new directions, and some may choose to find a more comfortable place for worship. This is not an easy journey.

In this small room next to a valley that used to be a sea, it's impossible to avoid my own doubts, fears and anxieties. There is nowhere to go, no television or telephone, no movie theater for miles, no distractions except the deer wandering outside my window. Yesterday it snowed; it's cold and the only sound is the sizzling of sappy wood in the fireplace. The warmth and beauty of that hearth tug at my longings.

My inner hearth is harder to see, less accessible and sometimes cold. Here I'm confronted with my own small world, my hidebound ways of thinking and seeing. I want to run, to find something to do or someone to talk to, music to listen to, something to avoid turning my gaze inward. I'd have to walk through too much fresh snow to get to my car. I'm stuck. I am my own shark in a tank of my creation.

If we're honest, we all live in tanks of our own making. To be sure, some tanks are smaller, some bigger, but all are made of glass which makes them hard to see from the inside out. Perhaps it's time for an objective view. We need a prophetic mirror to help us see ourselves as we are without our self-imposed blinders.

The risen Christ is often found outside the gate looking in and seeing us as we are. What is he saying to you and to your church?

We do not fear, for we believe God dreams
of worlds we can't conceive.

—*Thomas Troeger*

Brad Berglund
Advent, 2000
The Carmelite Monastery
Crestone, Colorado

Acknowledgments

THROUGHOUT MY JOURNEY, MANY PEOPLE HAVE been mentors and colleagues for me. I want to express my deep gratitude to the following people.

To my family for creating the time and space I needed to complete this manuscript. Rita for your grace, Brandon for your courage, and Brianna for your love—I am forever grateful.

To my parents, Edythe and Howard Berglund, the best model of partners in ministry I've ever known. Thanks, Dad, for the integrity of worship I experienced growing up in your congregation.

To J. Eugene Wright, professor and ministry colleague, who introduced me to the academic world of worship studies and made those studies come to life in worship.

To D. George Vanderlip, professor and ministry colleague, who encouraged my desire to plan and lead worship.

To LaRue A. Loughhead. Larry, for your challenging theology and unwavering devotion to thoughtful worship, I am in your debt.

To Mary Armacost Hulst, gifted preacher and long-time colleague. Mary, many of our creative collaborations are reflected in the ideas expressed in this book.

To Theodorre Donson and Kathy Hurley for friendship and love. Ted, your precise editing of my manuscript and tender-hearted encouragement made this book possible. Kathy, for being so much like me but always a step ahead, courageously blazing the trail toward personal transformation—thank you.

And to Susan and Robert Davis, new ministry colleagues, for your vision, creativity and commitment to God's unending surprises, I offer you my heart-felt thanks.

Introduction

WE FELT SMALL. IT'S HARD TO FEEL ANYTHING else when you're seated in the nave of a cathedral squinting up at pointed arches, buttressed walls and magnificent stained glass. Just a few years before we were high school friends talking about the meaning of life over a bowl of ice cream. Now, Rebecca, a newly ordained Episcopal priest, and I sat together pondering the mysteries of life and waiting for the Ash Wednesday procession to begin.

As the silent line of robed celebrants brushed my left arm, the man with a long stick leading the way caught my attention. I tilted my head just enough to breathe aloud, "Who's that?"

After an appropriate pause, she leaned just enough to say in a long loud whisper, "He's the verger."

Following a dignified moment, my curiosity got the best of me. I tilted again and asked, "What's he do?"

Another pause. The cross was passing. Her eyes never left the chancel. She leaned closer this time. "He gets rid of the sheep."

This time, a longer pause. I gave an inquisitive nod and blurted out softly, "You have problems with sheep here?"

Truth is, a hundred years ago in rural England, the answer to that question was, "Yes, we do." Now, the verger with staff in hand still clears the way but for different reasons and through a cleaner aisle.

This scene illustrates how a practical custom has taken on new symbolic meaning mostly hidden to the casual worshiper. Rebecca was obviously making a point to teach me something about the procession. I got the point.

There is often a need in our life for a clearing away of the dirt

Liturgy

[The word] liturgy ... has a secular origin. Its origin is the Greek leitourgia, *composed from words for work (*érgon*) and people (*laós*). In ancient Greece, a liturgy was a public work, something performed for the benefit of the city or state. Its principle was the same as that for paying taxes, but it could involve donated service as well as taxes. Paul speaks of the Roman authorities literally as "liturgists of God" (Romans 13:6) and of himself as "a liturgist of Christ Jesus to the Gentiles" (Romans 15:16).*

Liturgy, then, is a work performed by the people for the benefit of others. In other words, it is the quintessence of the priesthood of all believers in which the whole priestly community of Christians shares. To call a service "liturgical" is to indicate that it was conceived so that all worshipers take an active part in offering their worship together.

James F. White
Introduction to Christian Worship, 23-24.

and debris in our minds and hearts to make room for the gospel. Thanks to Rebecca, the verger has become an important symbol of preparation for me. But not all worshipers are blessed, as I was that day, with a priest in their pocket to help interpret what's going on in worship. Even in the free-church tradition in which churches emphasize making worship accessible, the outsider needs to be given the secrets of the inner sanctum. Even when the liturgy doesn't come from a prayer book, those who worship at any church each week know that liturgy by heart. We must keep our liturgy fresh and vibrant by always looking for new meaning in our familiar forms and actions.

Reinventing Sunday is intended to be an inspirational, practical resource for those leading worship on a regular basis. When you are planning and leading worship, seven days go by quickly. Because I know the pressure of that routine, it's my heart's desire that this book will not only relieve some pressure but will support you in breathing life into your weekly ritual. I also hope that the ideas and suggestions expressed here will fuel dialogue at your worship committee meeting or pastoral staff retreat.

Many of the ideas in this book are already permanent fixtures in some churches. In many ways, worship is not created; it is discovered and recreated. My discoveries come from excursions into a variety of denominational traditions: Lutheran, Episcopal, Roman Catholic, Baptist, Mennonite, Pentecostal, Orthodox, and others. I have also been deeply enriched by cultural traditions: Latino, African American, Asian, and my own Anglo-European tradition. For each of us, worship exists in the crucible of our own life context. The transformative potential to reinvent Sunday is found when an idea is liberated from the limitations of its own tradition and breaks through into a new worship environment.

The worldwide Christian family displays a rich tapestry of worship designs filled with spiritual depth and cultural energy. In our ever smaller global village, we are privileged to have diverse worship resources at our fingertips.

I approach the subject of Christian worship with some clear assumptions in mind. It will be best for both of us if you know what those assumptions are.

1. I believe worship should be offered to God as worship, not as evangelism or as Christian education.
2. Worship is what we, the worshipers, do for God.
3. Although many of the skills transfer, leading worship is not a performance. Leaders of worship prompt those in the pew to

offer their lives to God. They are skilled mediators of a cosmic drama between Creator and those created in the image of their Creator.

4. If we open our hearts to God's presence, worship can transform our lives and relationships and make us more trusting and faithful human beings.

5. Jesus asks us to love God with our heart, soul, mind and strength. Therefore, worship should activate our whole self, including our bodies.

6. Jesus also asks us to love our neighbor as ourselves. God-centered worship expands our souls, makes us generous, and sends us into the world to love and serve.

7. Like a weekly mini-pilgrimage, worship is an adventure, a journey into the unknown toward God. In that way, worship has flow and movement.

In the past few years, many worship leaders have been influenced by the work of Robert Webber. His emphasis on the four-fold movement of the liturgy has made an impact on my thinking and that impact is reflected here. I've organized this book according to that liturgical pattern: (1) gathering the people, (2) service of the Word, (3) responding in gratitude, (4) going out to serve. That does not mean the ideas here are limited to those who incorporate the four-fold approach. I have simply organized the material in that way.

Following this book's preface and introduction comes "The Prelude," which explores the lost art of preparation and offers some ideas for people and pastor to come into the sanctuary with anticipation and expectation. "Movement One: Gathering" includes the opening parts of the service: gathering, greeting, praising, singing, and praying. "Movement Two: Encountering" focuses on proclamation of the Word through Scripture and sermon. "Movement Three: Responding" looks at the variety of ways we can ask people to respond to God's love for them. This includes Communion, baptism, the offering, and the invitation to respond. "Movement Four: Embracing" explores ways to send our congregation into the world to love God by serving others.

"The Postlude" contains two chapters. Chapter 13 is "The Modulating Congregation." Using the analogy of musical modulation in which a musician moves from one key to another, this section describes the dissonance that changing keys creates and gives some proven methods for validating and working through the inevitable tensions that occur when we change our styles of worship. Chapter 14 is called "Cleaning Up." Here I respond to such questions as, "Where shall we put the children's story?" "What about the announcements?" "Is applause appropriate in worship?" These questions can bog down a worship committee and keep them focused away from the heart of the dialogue.

The appendixes offer other resources. The first explores the gift of liturgical time and contrasts the "Hallmark year" with the life of Jesus. Appendixes B, C, and D offer examples of thematic worship experiences outside the normal weekly gathering. These services could inspire our congregations to greater awareness of worship. These include a home dedication, a healing prayer service, and a worship service in the style of the Taizé community.

The Prelude

THE WORD *PRELUDE,* FROM THE LATIN *preludium,* means "to play before." In a worship service, the musical preludes can be a part of worship, but they also provide a moment of transition before worship. This moment is an opportunity for entering worshipers to prepare themselves for their unique journey into God's presence. For worshipers and worship leaders, the depth of their personal preparation for worship will determine the quality of the experience.

Those who lead the worship service have many responsibilities. Their preparation involves personal readiness to meet with God, but it also includes the details of leadership. That leadership preparation needs to be taken seriously, but as hard as many worship leaders work, for the worshiper in the pew, inner transformation does not depend on what the leader does. If individual participants prepare carefully to give the gift of themselves in worship, then the well-prepared worship leader need only support worshipers by making it easier to give that personal spiritual gift to God.

During the prelude, leaders and participants alike make a conscious shift from the outer landscape of weekly experience to the inner landscape of the heart, which is symbolized in the holiness of the sanctuary. Whether you are a worship leader or a worshiper, use the prelude to make that transition, and you will move beyond time and space and into the loving arms of the Creator of the universe.

Chapter 1

Understanding Worship

Worship, in all its grades and kinds,
is the response of the creature to the Eternal.

Evelyn Underhill, Worship, 3

OUR PEDIATRICIAN KNEW; SHE HAD TO. SHE HAD seen it all. I'm glad she didn't spill all those horrific beans at once. Looking into Brandon's eye told her what she needed to know.

"This could be a virus or a 'mass' in the brain." Sadness belied her professional, matter-of-fact tone.

"A mass?" I stumbled over the word.

So began the first step toward hearing the news no parent wants to imagine. As we sat with the pediatrician in that office, she was not saying and we weren't asking. Surely, we were bracing for the shock and despair that was coming. By four o'clock that afternoon, we were sitting with a neurologist in a small, dimly lit room, struggling to hear a diagnosis from hell.

"Your son has a very large tumor in the center of his brain. We're not sure yet if it's malignant but its shape makes that highly probable." He knew. It was spreading out with finger-like aggression. He knew. But I understand now why he didn't say it. At a deep level, we knew already. He didn't need to say it. Our four-year-old son could be dead in a few days. We walked out of the room and tried not to throw up.

After living for seven years in a "California Dream," we were moving to Denver, to a part of the country we both called home. Rita hailed from the western slope of Colorado and I from the middle of Kansas. I'd accepted a position in a wonderful church; my wife and I loved each other; our young son and daughter were beautiful and happy. I was in love with my life.

In pastoral ministry, I felt called to heal the hurts of others, to pray for their children and to bury their loved ones. Tragedy happened to others, and I was there to help them. I was important, confident and well respected.

Did I worship my life? That thought had never crossed my mind. Two short months later at Denver's Children's Hospital, I would have many new thoughts race through my mind.

Brandon's tumor was diagnosed on Monday. The first invasive procedure into his brain would be two days later. It lasted eleven hours. The surgeon was excellent, but the tumor didn't cooperate and part of it remained in the center of Brandon's brain. A fragile boy who needed to recover would have to start cancer treatments right away. The life I loved had slipped away.

That next Sunday, as Rita and I wept over our wounded son and our two-year-old daughter tried to figure out what was happening, I felt an overwhelming need to be in worship. I walked to a large, downtown church with a vaulted ceiling and beautiful, classic music. Hoping to vanish into the congregation in that crowded place, I knelt and let the transcendent architecture of the sanctuary wash over me.

In my small, shattered corner of the world, I tried to immerse myself in the expansiveness of that room, hoping desperately that God's view of my life was larger than mine. In the depth of my dark wood, in a place filled with grief and pain, in the loneliness of my fear and doubt, I looked up at the glory of God, and all I could do was whisper, "Help me."

4

Creative worship means using one's imagination and creativity. It means personal empowerment—using our own ability to create meaningful worship rather than relying on others to do it for us. It means being able to use material from within a tradition without being limited or constrained by it.

Dara Molloy, "Creative Worship in the
Celtic Tradition," in Celtic Threads, 105

I had taken my life to worship. The depth of my grief caused a reorientation of my understanding. For the first time, I understood—I stood under the power of worship. My crisis became an opportunity for me to reconsider its meaning.

Expanding Your Vision for Worship

It may be that churches also need a crisis to re-frame their approach to worship—a crisis such as dwindling attendance or apathetic involvement. A more effective motivation would be a desire for worshipers to be mature, deeply spiritual human beings.

For a local congregation, worship is the one time and place during the week when church members gather together for the sole purpose of offering their individual lives and church life to God. Churches schedule many other meetings, dinners, educational opportunities, service projects and programs. However, congregational worship is unique in its purpose. It is intended to be the opening ceremony, the foundational act that gives birth and meaning to all our other agendas. If we want to revitalize worship in our local church, we need to recognize what it really is: opening our hearts and offering our lives to God. Then worship will become the centerpiece of congregational life.

Ultimately, it is the responsibility of worshipers in the pew to open their hearts and offer their lives to God. No one can do that for them. Having said that, it is equally true that the prompters of worship, the leaders on the platform, have a responsibility to offer effective and varied avenues of worship so participants can respond in fresh ways.

Think of those avenues of participation—singing, praying, Scripture reading and so on—as a window in a cabin on a lake. In an attempt to see the sky—to experience God—worshipers look through that window and see, let's say, one goose flying by. If that window is small, the experience is small—one goose on a spot of blue sky and a few leaves on the branch of a nearby tree. By expanding the possibilities for participation in worship, leaders have the opportunity to transform a small portal into a large bay window where worshipers realize that the sky is filled with geese, the cabin is next to a beautiful forest of trees, and the blue sky is dotted with white puffs of clouds. Their view of reality has just taken an enormous shift.

Creativity in worship isn't about making change for change's sake. Rather, we realize that, like a dark cabin with a window that is too small, our current resources for worship may be stale, dark, and undersized for the longings of our souls. For some worshipers, our liturgy may be a tiny porthole with one small fish swimming by. The worship leader's task is to throw open the windows of eternity and allow the congregation to put their heads through and be transformed by an expansive view of God.

Recognizing the Hindrances to Worship
In his book *The Fifth Discipline*, systems thinker Peter M. Senge has taken organizational thinking to a new, or fifth, dimension. The implications of his insights could have a dramatic and life-giving effect on local congregations.

First, Senge says we all have mental models that we bring to any situation. He describes these models as "deeply ingrained assumptions, generalizations, or even pictures or images that influence how we understand the world and how we take action" *(Fifth*

Metaphors for God
At different stages in our lives one metaphor may elucidate God more fully than others ... [but] when we overuse one metaphor or one set of metaphors, we are in fact leaning into heresy. Sovereign metaphors for God, for instance, emphasizing kingship, thrones, majesty and judgment, may be true. But overused, they become not only irrelevant (when did you last, in your daily life, bow before a throne?), they become heretical, as they give an incomplete (and therefore false) picture of what God is like. ... Still, we certainly need many metaphors to even begin to understand someone as great and wonderful as God.

Mary Ellen Ashcroft, Dogspell, 12

Discipline, 8). For worshipers that idea might translate to mental models we have about God.

One of these constructs might be "God is male," which results in seeing God as a father figure. Another might be "God is not male," which is often a reaction against the traditional construct. From a more objective point of view, biblically speaking, we affirm that God is, by nature, both masculine and feminine and at the same time beyond our categories of gender.

So, the real question might be, who is God? That could be a transformative question to bring in your heart as you come to worship.

Opening to New Possibilities

Understanding where our mental models originate is important spiritual and therapeutic work. If worshipers spend time in spiritual direction and personal devotion during the week, they might discover where their mental models originate and might learn skills to expand their models and become freer human beings.

This work is what Senge would refer to as personal mastery. He uses the term mastery not to suggest gaining dominance over people or things but as a special level of proficiency. People who ask fundamental questions about their deeply ingrained assumptions and discover limitations in their own personalities and attitudes are developing personal mastery by asking a fundamentally spiritual question, "Who am I?"

Most of us know the prayer by St. Francis of Assisi called "Lord, Make Me an Instrument of Your Peace." We pray it as a request for transformation and renewal. Franciscan priest and retreat director Richard Rohr tells us there is a lesser-known prayer of St. Francis that could transform us even more deeply. Father Rohr says that St. Francis sat in his cell and repeated the prayer, "Lord, who are you and who am I?"

Imagine genuinely wanting to explore the answer to those questions and coming to worship with that prayer on our own lips. The person who follows the example set by St. Francis experiences worship as a voyage of discovery.

The dictionary defines the word *create* as "to cause to exist; bring into being." The word *innovate* comes from the Latin root *novus* meaning "fresh" or "new." It is related to the word *ovary* and speaks of the mystery of fertility and birth. So creativity in worship isn't about making our church more special or asking an elite group of artists to "do their thing." It is fundamentally about the act of birthing a new creation. Understanding or standing under the power of worship includes finding ways to activate all the avenues of the senses. Then worshipers can give birth to their deep longings for God and be drawn into a more complete awareness of God's nature.

The catechism of the Episcopal Church asks the question, "Why do we praise God?" The answer is simple and profound: "We praise God, not to obtain anything, but because God's being

Awareness

People come together in organizations for, in some sense, a noble purpose, but are finding ways to constrict or even destroy life in the process. And when we really probe deeply into that way of organizing, we'll find ourselves. It's where we'll find our own fears and anxieties and beliefs played out. We won't find somebody behind the curtain who's causing it to happen.

Peter M. Senge, in an interview
with Margaret Wheatley, 33

draws praise from us." It is up to worship leaders to create innovative ways to open the windows of heaven and invite the congregation to walk through. Perhaps then worshipers will be free in body, mind and spirit to respond to God's invitation.

Keys to Developing a Creative Environment for Worship

1. Create a web of learning. One of the ways to develop creativity is to experience creativity. Worship leaders who do not experience worship outside their own environment are limited to their own designs, traditions and personal church experience.

One way to develop a learning environment is for churches to invite the pastor who plans the liturgy to visit other services of worship in a variety of denominations. For example, the fifth Sunday of the month could be used as an expeditionary Sunday. Exploring other worship services four Sundays a year provides a way to share in and bring home the creativity of others. Churches who implemented this practice would create an ecumenical "web of learning" that might eventually lead congregations to cooperative ventures with other churches. In our cynical world, *coopetition*—the understanding that churches are unique but work together to fulfill Christ's mission on earth—rather than *competition* might begin to heal religious divisions.

2. Nurture a worship team. A worship team is different from a "praise team." If your congregation does not have a worship committee or a worship leadership team, it is time to start one. Beyond regular prayer for worship, this group needs education in worship, both its design and implementation. In addition to this book, there are many resources available for worship education. The worship team needs to be free to experiment with a variety of styles and approaches to worship. In this laboratory setting, a church staff could identify those lay participants who desire innovation in worship and are gifted for worship leadership.

In addition, it would serve a church to send this group out on Sundays to other churches. Participation in a variety of worship settings is refreshing. Saturday outings will include Seventh-day Adventists and various Jewish communities.

3. Become a school of the Spirit. One of the views most compatible with Christianity in the book *The Fifth Discipline* is the idea of developing a learning organization. Just as Jesus developed a community of spiritual growth among his disciples, church leaders are called to create an environment of growth for their congregations.

However, pastors are too often constricted by an unfortunate assumption that contradicts this goal. It goes something like this: "I've been hired and am paid by this congregation to provide quality leadership. My education prepared me to offer authoritative and professional guidance and wisdom to this church. That's what I'm here to do."

On the surface, this assumption seems reasonable and obvious to anyone in pastoral ministry. However, the dilemma occurs when you activate it. The congregation sits back and watches while the pastor lives out his or her sincere devotion to doing a good job. Church members live busy lives, so their

> *Inclusive Worship*
> *Worship is too important to be left to the experts. All must be involved, for all participate and are deeply affected by it.*
> *... the worship committee must be open to consultations with a ten year old child. Adults think differently than do children, and often they forget how children perceive worship and participate in it.*
>
> David Ng and Virginia Thomas
> Children in the Worshiping Community, *114, 119*

posture of passive receptivity also seems reasonable.

Peter Senge suggests that the real, though hidden, work of any leader is to create a learning environment in which people realize their wisdom is an essential part of what is being created. This is different than the all too common, "make them think it was their idea" approach to leadership because it creates a shared vision.

This new leadership style involves the entire church in creating a "relational child," a unique future that will only emerge with shared dialogue and cooperative implementation. In this visionary setting, Senge suggests parking our roles at the door because the new and only role of "the leader" is to ensure that each person's wisdom is heard.

In the church, our reason for listening is our belief that every baptized person is a temple of the Holy Spirit. Learning to listen needs to begin with the church staff in its internal relationships. A professional staff that among its own ranks models covenant leadership—leadership that is not authoritarian but that respects and draws out the unique gifts of each staff member—can then extend that style of leadership to the congregation. A movement like this could transform our churches.

Chapter 2

Starting on Purpose:
The Lost Art of Preparation

To the arriving and leaving. To the journey.
I wake to the freshness. And do reverence.

—*Jack Gilbert, in* Monolithos

DURING THE YEARS 950 TO 1200 C.E., HUNDREDS of thousands of people around Europe were on the move. These weren't two week family vacations. This was pilgrimage—an excursion on foot that would stretch the limits of the strongest person. Charged with all the meaning of life and death, a personal pilgrimage was often dangerous and always strenuous. Potentially, it was the last act of a person's life.

People went for a variety of reasons. Some traveled to fulfill a vow. Others were doing penance for sins committed. Still others went for spiritual renewal and hope. Many wanted to be in a sacred site associated with a holy person. There were those who thought a pilgrimage would earn them favor in the next life and others who wanted to test their courage.

They went to a variety of places such as Jerusalem, Rome, Santiago de Compostela, and Canterbury. Associated with mystery,

Pilgrimages have been an important part of religious history throughout the ages. A pilgrimage is a ritual journey with a hallowed purpose. Every step along the way has meaning. The pilgrim knows that the journey will be difficult and that life-giving challenges will emerge. A pilgrimage is not a vacation; it is a transformational journey during which significant change takes place. New insights are given. Deeper understanding is attained. New and old places in the heart are visited. Blessings are received. Healing takes place. On return from the pilgrimage, life is seen with different eyes. Nothing will ever be quite the same again.

Macrina Wiederkehr,
Behold Your Life, 11

saints, the stories of Jesus, martyrdom, or miracles, these holy places became symbolic of the journey of life toward some finality on earth and eternity with God.

Before leaving on a journey of this magnitude, pilgrims were given a ceremony of "leave-taking." Often in the form of a mass at the local parish church, specific rituals of blessing gave the pilgrim strength and courage for the long road ahead. This ceremony gave appropriate recognition and importance to the transforming possibilities in that person's life.

In our day, pilgrimage is once again gaining in popularity. In our high tech world, perhaps there is a deepening need for meaning. Just by reading modern books and magazines, it's easy to see that people today are more global and internationally sophisticated than previous generations, but business and entertainment travel is apparently wearing thin. In their longing for divine connection,

> *Pilgrims are poets who create by taking journeys.*
> *Richard R. Niebuhr, quoted in*
> The Art of Pilgrimage *by Phil Cousineau, 13*

people are discovering that time apart from routines and business pressure is necessary. A different quality of time is needed to heal our wounds, listen deeply to our lives, and hear the voice of God.

Through pilgrimage, many people are rediscovering the transforming possibilities of the three-fold movement of all-spiritual discipline—intentional preparation and leaving, mindful or transformative experience, and re-entry or integration. This pattern is a natural part of the spiritual practice of pilgrimage and is what makes pilgrimage different from other travel opportunities.

Worship as Pilgrimage

This three-fold pattern is also the natural movement of communal worship. Like a weekly mini- pilgrimage, worship is an adventure, a journey into the unknown toward God. In this way, worship has flow and movement that needs to become personal.

Like a pilgrimage, this journey is not to be taken lightly. If worship is to be a transformational act, it needs thoughtful preparation, mindful experience, and purposeful reintegration. However, in our fast-paced society, the rituals of preparation are often overlooked. Yet without them, we come to worship with our minds racing, our bodies overworked, and our emotions confused by the events of daily life.

The following suggestions focus on personal preparation for communal worship. Many of the ideas expressed here come from traditions associated with Sabbath keeping. While the concept of "Sabbath time" has a broader application than one day of the week, we can assume here that a Sabbath Day or "day of rest" is a specific day that has as its focal point the gathering of the congregation for worship.

Sabbath Keeping

How long has it been since you've heard these familiar words, "Remember the Sabbath day to keep it holy." In countless ways, the fourth commandment from Exodus 20 seems impossible to keep in the modern era. The Gospel of Mark records Jesus' words, "The Sabbath was made for humanity, and not humanity for the Sabbath" (Mark 2:27, *The Unvarnished Gospels*). We read this statement and breathe a sigh of relief. But if we look deeper, we'll see that Jesus is simply turning the Sabbath from law into gift.

As a law, the idea of *Shabbat*—to cease, desist, or rest—was not to be taken lightly. Numbers 15:32-36 says if a man was found gathering wood on the Sabbath contrary to the Lord's command, he was to be stoned to death by the community. The message of that ancient society is clear—stop working or die. It is also the opposite of modern society's message, which is "stop working *and* die."

Just as clear is Jesus' message. He asks us to choose the gift of grace—to recognize on our own that taking time to rest and occupy our thoughts with the things of God is good for body and soul. Sabbath is a quality of time that can restore, heal and transform. It is a gift worth receiving.

In order to deepen our worship experience, preparation for the

Sabbath

The Sabbath is a day of delightful communion with God and one another.... Joyful observance of this holy time from evening to evening, sunset to sunset, is a celebration of God's creative and redemptive acts.

Seventh-day Adventists Believe ..., 248

We're often admonished to stay away from "mindless ritual" but rarely encouraged, in its place, to create "mindful ritual." Ritual simply allows us to coax meaning from our inner world by giving it form in the outer world. In this way, we don't create meaning. We evoke meaning.

Brad Berglund

experience of worship is crucial. Without proper preparation, the normal onslaught of details, distractions and routines will soon creep in and occupy our time. Preparation will allow us to clear away the complications of life by systematically putting them aside in order to simplify the hours around worship. This freedom of simplicity will allow us to focus our attention and come to worship with anticipation. If we can put worship in the context of an entire Sabbath "container"—that specific period of time each week during which we focus on God and unhook from the busyness of life—we will find our worship even more satisfying and renewing. Either way, the following ideas will guide you and the congregation.

Personal Preparation for Worship

Set aside the evening before worship to create meaningful ritual. Jewish tradition offers practical ideas here. The following suggestions may be used alone or as a way to structure an entire evening. Make this evening a special event for family and friends.

- ❖ Establish a special dinner the evening before you worship. Consider preparing food that has meaning and memory for each person present.
- ❖ Dress for this occasion.
- ❖ Make the setting important by using your best place settings and tablecloth.
- ❖ Carefully ritualize candle lighting (three candles symbolizing

our triune God) and blessings to each person present.

❖ Read a psalm or other Scripture and express gratitude to God for the gift of life.

❖ Bless the food with an eye toward worship and remembering Christ in our midst. "Whenever you do this, do it in remembrance of me."

❖ After dinner, spend time talking about the events of the past week. Give each person a chance to express something for which they are grateful and something that has caused them anxiety or pain.

❖ Before dessert, as those present turn their attention to the next day's worship, give each one time with the following questions (adapted from the book *Behold Your Life* by Macrina Wiederkehr, 15):

■ Am I beginning this journey with an open heart? In what way?

■ Is there a part of me that has closed the door to God right now? Which part?

■ Do I fear this journey to God in any way? Can I name those fears?

■ Is there a door that needs to be opened so that I can experience worship more fully?

■ Is there someone in my faith community who has hurt me? Does that relationship need to be reconciled?

■ Is there someone I have hurt? Do I need to ask for forgiveness?

❖ Personally prepare for your day of worship by bathing the night before and setting out your clothing for the next morning. When you awaken, this will increase the simplicity of your focus before worship. If you have small children, taking care of your own details first will give you added strength to attend to their needs.

Set aside thirty minutes before you leave for worship service to read the Scriptures of the day and spend time in prayer. For busy people—especially pastors, church musicians, church-school teachers and parents of young children—this suggestion will prompt an

> *In an increasing number of Christian lives the last vestige of the Christian sabbath is a quick hour on Sunday mornings sandwiched between the Sunday paper and a busy afternoon, and even this hour has disappeared for many. Sunday is fast becoming just another day to maintain ego focus and mastery, and to make money and spend it, in an increasingly privatized life.*
>
> *Tilden Edwards,* Sabbath Time, *15*

outburst of laughter. But before you dismiss it, give it a chance. Think about it. All week long we rush around trying to accomplish the day-to-day work of life. Bringing a sense of resolve and commitment to making the day of worship different is a challenging but rewarding task. Exchanging stressful details and routines with your own focused preparation will have a dramatic effect on your level of anticipation as you enter worship.

Churchwide Preparation for Worship

Develop a tradition to prepare for special seasons of the liturgical year. For example, you could use the following suggestions for the Lenten season.

❖ The Tuesday evening before Ash Wednesday is a good time to offer a special evening of preparation for the Lenten season. Traditionally, this evening has been seen as a time to overindulge before the rigors of Lent set in—hence the name, "Mardi Gras" or Fat Tuesday. But the dictionary says the origin of Lent is Middle English and means "spring." Originally Lent was not so much about fasting or denial as it is about welcoming the new life of Easter!

❖ Instead of an extreme experience, make the evening before Ash Wednesday a balanced, fun evening by focusing on the "feasting" aspects of Lent. We only fast in order to feast. Fast from idle gossip, feast on the goodness of others; fast from pessimism, feast on optimism; fast from criticism, feast on affirmation; fast from judging others, feast on Christ dwelling in them; and so on.

❖ Decorate the sanctuary for Lent. Not only is this a good way to involve the congregation in preparing for this important season of the church year, it would include them in re-creating their own worship space. Hands-on preparation for worship will raise their level of anticipation for worship and unite the congregation in service to one another.

❖ Create a devotional booklet for the days of Lent. This is an effective way for members of the congregation to offer spiritual insight and guidance to each other. It will also increase a sense of community during the Lenten season that will spill over into worship. Early in January, invite members of your worship committee and church board to write one devotional each using a story from their life based on the theme of personal devotion to God. Before they write, give them an example of the format and an example of a well-written devotion (such as the one on page 20). Make sure their name is included with their writing. Hand this devotional booklet out to the congregation at your Mardi Gras celebration.

An example of a Lenten devotional:

The "Via Negativa"

During the last ten years I have learned in a deep way that the path of spiritual transformation involves a process of embracing suffering, death, and rebirth. Unlike the butterfly, which we observe going through one major metamorphosis, human beings can choose with awareness to continually be open and matured by the sorrows and losses that life inevitably brings. During our years of living in the hospital, I was privileged to walk alongside several children and adults as they faced death and as some went through the dying process. There were remarkable individuals who faced death with great skill, maturity, and intention, while others struggled painfully and suffered with unresolved relationships.

From these experiences I learned how important it was to come to terms, not only with the possibility of Brandon's death, but with my own death as well. It has produced a powerful desire to live each day with great gratitude, awareness, and clarity. Suffering, grief, loss, as well as joy, are important teachers. I have learned that God's work is often most powerful and most loving in the darkest of nights.

In the traditions of Christian spiritual formation, this learning from the darkness is called the "via negativa," or dark night of the soul. Lent has come to be an invitation in my own life to do the important work of grieving and letting go of all that holds me back so that I may be open to the spiritual rebirthing that God promises with every spring.

"Deep calls to deep in the roar of your waterfalls; all your waves and breakers have swept over me. By day the LORD directs his love, at night his song is with me—a prayer to the God of my life." (Psalm 42:7–8, NIV)

Rita Berglund, February 2000

Movement 1
Gathering

ONE OF MY FONDEST CHILDHOOD MEMORIES is of yearly vacations with my family. For at least two weeks every summer, our family piled into the station wagon and headed across country. With my lead-footed father at the wheel, my observant mother navigating, and my brother playing cards at my side, we had visited half of the fifty states by the time I was fifteen. Some summers found us in muggy Philadelphia, others in windy South Dakota. Once in a while we escaped the plains of Kansas to enjoy the cool air of the Colorado Rockies.

Now that I have children of my own, I desire to create the same kinds of positive family memories. As I mine my childhood family treasure chest for gems of wisdom, the consistent theme that emerges from those summer excursions is the intention with which my parents planned, prepared, and ritualized our going.

We counted off the days on the family calendar. We discussed the trip in detail. A group of friends made travel baskets filled with games, snacks, candy, and daily surprises to be opened as we drove. The car was packed the night before. Plants were watered, friends called, mail held, dog delivered, newspaper stopped—check, check, check. The anticipation was excruciating.

Finally, after a near sleepless night, in the cool darkness, we shuffled out to the car for an early morning departure. But there was one more piece of the ritual, the final act that would make it possible to finally drive down the driveway.

Before we left, my parents turned toward the back seat and asked us to bow our heads. In that quiet moment, our preparation, anticipation, and excitement was swept up into the unknown of the adventure that lay ahead of us.

That simple moment of ritualized transition put our vacation in context. It created a bracket that would set those two weeks apart from everyday life. It announced to each of us the obvious but often overlooked truth that something completely new was about to happen. It was the signal that it was time to go. So at 5:00 A.M., my parents offered prayers of blessing for our journey, Dad started the car, I waved at my room, and we were off.

As I look back on my childhood, I can see now that those oft-ritualized departures became part of a pattern that would add to the strength I needed as an eighteen year old leaving for college, never to return in the same way.

Chapter 3

Gathering and Greeting

*Out of need and out of custom
we have gathered here again,
to the gathering we are bringing
love and laughter, grief and pain.
Some believing, some rejoicing,
some afraid and some in doubt.
Come we now our questions voicing,
we would search these matters out.*

Ken Medema, "The Gathering"

THESE LYRICS FROM KEN MEDEMA'S "THE GATH-
ering" describe the gathering of God's people for worship. Listen to the action: gathering, bringing, believing, rejoicing,
voicing, searching. This is not a passive group of spectators.
These are active people bringing their fears, doubts, grief, joy,
faith and questions to worship—honest people in need of
authentic experience.

I experience that authenticity most vividly when I venture into
a monastic worship setting. Here I find people who live, work,
play, and pray together. They are well acquainted with one

another's needs, joys, and hurts. There is an abiding sense of community, easily felt and silently entered into. Here, there is no welcome committee at the front door, no organ prelude, few instructions for the visitor. Those who enter find it a quiet, hallowed place that honors simplicity.

By contrast, a large southern California church that I visited a few years ago has thousands of members, and a third of their worshiping congregation each week are visitors. How would worship leaders ever create a sense of community in that setting? I was surprised to discover how well they had solved that problem.

From the moment people entered the church, reverberations from a large pipe organ created a vibrant atmosphere. Greeters at the door were friendly and informative. People chatted freely as they entered, finding an empty seat before those seats disappeared.

In the midst of that exciting hubbub, I discovered yet another welcome surprise. Throughout the sanctuary, robed worship leaders were walking the aisles shaking hands and greeting those who had found a seat. Cordially welcoming visitors and checking in with members, they created a genuine sense of warmth that was palpable. Here were leaders who knew their setting and made the best of it.

Gathering your congregation with intentionality creates an atmosphere of expectation and anticipation for worship that will carry through the entire experience.

Suggestions for Worshipers

1. Come with awareness and honesty. Gathering for worship is not for the faint of heart. We're coming to meet with the Creator of the universe, to plumb the depths of our own spirits and to celebrate Christ in our midst. This gathering has everything to do with the ultimate meaning and purpose of our lives. Let it be deep. Allow God to touch your emotions as well as your mind. Make it a time of renewal and fulfillment. Expect your life to be changed.

Step one is to be aware of your own thoughts and feelings. In

Come we now our masks displaying
fearing that we shall be known
foolish games forever playing
feeling meanwhile so alone
Let pretension's power be broken
to be human let us dare
let the truth in love be spoken
let us now the questing share.

Ken Medema, "The Gathering"

order to give the gift of yourself, you'll need to know yourself as you are in that moment. Take time to be honest with yourself.

2. Look for someone new. As you gather, look for a new and unfamiliar face. Take the initiative to greet someone you've never met. A church's capacity to love and serve its community is directly proportional to its members' ability to befriend visitors one at a time.

3. Once you've entered the sanctuary, observe silence. We live in a world of sporting events, theater, and concerts. Our normal pattern is to sit down and talk to those around us as we wait for the show to begin. In worship, a sanctuary has replaced the arena, participants have replaced spectators and pastors have replaced celebrities. We have all come to focus on God. Observing silence as we enter the sanctuary gives our hearts a chance to catch up with our busy lives, and thus helps prepare us for worship.

4. Pray for those around you. Rather than talking to the people seated around you, pray silently for them. Each person carries a unique burden. As worship begins, bear each other's burdens by offering them to God.

5. Kneel in the presence of God. One of the Greek words frequently used for *worship* in the New Testament is the word *proskuneîn*, which describes the physical act of falling down. The

English translation is "prostrate." Bowing, kneeling, or bending a knee will give reverence and awe a foothold in your heart.

Suggestions for Worship Leaders

1. Create an atmosphere of reverence. Using the Old Testament temple as a model, move people from the outer court to the inner court and into the Holy of Holies. If you want people to enter the sanctuary in silence, strategically place your greeting staff with that sense of movement in mind. Make the outer doors of the church the place for excitement and welcoming by putting greeters there. Make the foyer the inner court—a quieter place where another group of helpers mingles in silence. A nametag with "may I help" or other functional designation allows visitors to ask them questions. Signs at the sanctuary doors inviting worshipers to enter in silence communicates that they are entering the Holy of Holies. Direct your ushers to give the printed order of service to worshipers in silence and with a smile.

2. If people enter in silence, offer them guided reflection. In addition to the printed bulletin, ask ushers to hand out a prayer card with a meditative image, a verse of Scripture or a set of questions. These promptings for prayer could be specifically chosen for the theme of the day's service, for the liturgical season of the year, or for general reflection on the relationship between life and worship. As the congregation gathers, give them five minutes of silence to reflect on this image or verse. When they are finished, have them stand and sing a song of assurance and joy.

3. Create an atmosphere of joy and celebration. Beginning twenty minutes before the opening call to worship, create an atmosphere of joy with lively music and praise songs. As the congregation enters the building for worship, ushers cordially greet them at the door. The enthusiasm will continue as they near the sanctuary because music and singing are drawing them into an atmosphere of praise. As the call to worship approaches, songs that are more reflective support worshipers in making a transition from praise to worship.

We have heard the glowing story
of the thing which God has done
of his power and his glory
of his love in Christ his son
God of human transformation
for your presence now we pray
lead us ever on the journey
as we gather here today.

Ken Medema, "The Gathering"

4. If your congregation talks during the prelude, join them. Rather than try to change a congregational pattern, worship leaders can come into the sanctuary and walk the aisles greeting those who've gathered for worship. In this atmosphere of warmth and greeting, the congregation feels welcome and makes a connection with those who are leading worship. Use recorded music during this time of talking and greeting. At the end of this period, call the congregation to attention and give them a formal invitation to greet each other and register their attendance. Then, using your church musicians, make a transition into a call to worship.

5. Affirm the awesome presence of God. People have often been admonished to "fear the Lord," but the biblical word we have translated as "fear" is better rendered as "awe." Direct people's attention to the awesome power of God through your call to worship. Make the opening moments a movement into that awesome power. Give a call to worship that is short and focused on the almighty and eternal nature of God. This call to worship can be either responsive or spoken by the leader.

Chapter 4

Praising and Singing

What we do in liturgy is too vast and too deep to be left to our speaking voices. We need music so that we can fully express what we are about.

Joseph Cardinal Bernardin,
in The Collegeville Hymnal, 7

THE ABBEY OF ST. WALBURGA IS A REMOTE OUT-post twenty miles south of the Wyoming border in northern Colorado. Of course, its isolated location is what makes it attractive as a place of retreat and spiritual renewal. It is home to twenty-five Sisters living a communal life under a Benedictine rule. So in addition to farming, raising cattle, studying Scripture, and receiving guests, that means they sing common prayer throughout their day. For Benedict, work and worship were equal services in the eyes of God.

The gentleness of their singing is enhanced by the beauty of their chapel set in a rugged valley of ponderosa pines with outcroppings of granite. Their patroness is a German saint, so they wear traditional European habits which gives visitors the sense that they have found a kind of "Sound of Music" for the American West.

These Benedictine sisters literally live "by the clock," gathering in the chapel six times a day to sing their prayer and offer their lives to God. Through these monastic offices, Benedict provided a scheme to sing systematically the entire Psalter each week. The vibrant acoustical environment of their worship space is ideal for their sung liturgy. Throughout a forty-five minute vesper service, the only spoken word is the reading of Scripture. Singing is their way of life.

Local churches are not monasteries and cannot pretend to be. However, there are lessons about worship to be learned from those who live a communal life and sing together six times a day in a church setting.

A Brief History of Singing in the Christian Church

The earliest groupings of Christian worshipers were Jewish in their traditions and worship styles. They brought psalm singing to their newfound faith in Christ. This chant-like singing was the early version of our church music. Protestant-style Christian worship as we know it today would have been unrecognizable to those early Christians.

As an expanding Christian movement took shape across the Middle East and Europe, hierarchical structures formed, and church leaders attempted to standardize worship. In the early third century, Hippolytus, a presbyter in the church of Rome, wrote a document describing seven daily hours of private prayer. It was a demanding routine that structured the day around the passion and death of Christ. Then, in the fourth century, the Roman Emperor Constantine gave his blessing to a growing Christian movement that meant greater freedom for the institutionalization of patterns and structures.

As hermit monks began living together in communities, this pattern of praying throughout the day became known as the monastic office. Benedict, writing in the sixth century, created his Rule for monastic life that includes guidelines for praying and singing that office. Later in the sixth century, the monastic psalm singing of those early monasteries was standardized under the leadership of Pope Gregory the Great. Since then, this style of psalm singing has been referred to as Gregorian chant.

From the sixth to the fourteenth centuries, monastic cities and their structured daily patterns formed the backbone of European life. During these Middle Ages, religion and worship were in the hands of professionally religious people who sang Gregorian chant. Local residents would come to church to "observe" mass being sung by the monastic choir. Much like sending a shirt to the dry cleaner to be washed, the peasant population of Europe would send their prayers to the monasteries to be prayed. Worship was something done on behalf of the common people.

Congregational Singing

Congregational singing, as we know it, is relatively new. The person who had the greatest single impact on the history of Western European church music was a young man from Germany named Martin Luther. Luther entered an Augustinian monastery on July 17, 1505 to become a monk. Two years later, he was ordained a priest. Then, in 1508 Luther took the post of professor of philosophy at Wittenberg University.

The sale of indulgences as a pardon for sins by Johann Tetzel at a church near Wittenberg incited Luther to do something that would change the course of church history. On October 31, 1517, he nailed his Ninety-Five Theses to the Castle Church door at Wittenberg. Luther was eventually excommunicated by the Roman church, and out of his protest an entirely new branch of Christianity was formed called the "protest" or Protestant church.

Luther was a highly skilled musician who played the lute and recorder. As a way of expressing the importance of participation in worship, he created congregational hymns, sometimes borrowing from the classical ensemble music of his day.

Some would have us believe that Martin Luther used popular German drinking songs as the basis of some of his hymns. This belief is promoted in order to justify the singing of rock music in

> ### Music
> *Next to the Word of God, the noble art of music is the greatest treasure in the world. It controls our thoughts, minds, hearts, and spirits. A person who does not regard music as a marvelous creation of God, must be a clodhopper indeed and does not deserve to be called a human being; he should be permitted to hear nothing but the braying of asses and the grunting of hogs.*
>
> Martin Luther, "Foreword," in Symphoniae

worship services. However, there are better arguments for using popular music in worship, and this theory about Luther's borrowing practices is historically dubious. The musical forms Luther borrowed were not from the local tavern.

Because Luther was passionate in his desire that people be involved in worship, he essentially gave the gift of congregational singing to the church. To be sure, European Christians were singing in worship before Luther—for example, Jan Huss and the Anabaptists (this group published its first hymnal in 1504 in the Czech language). But it was Luther who came from within the ranks of the established church and re-framed its entire approach to worship.

Suggestions for Cultivating Your Congregational Choir

1. Since the congregation is the choir, rehearse them before the service. Singing is the primary way a congregation offers its praise to God. Regular rehearsal with worshipers will help them accept their role as active participants in worship. If the music is unfamiliar to them, the song may be a frustration and hinder their ability to praise. If you are introducing a new song in worship, be sure to rehearse it with the congregation before worship begins. This will reduce their anxiety, and they will appreciate knowing the words and the melody before they sing it in worship.

2. Maintain the dramatic flow of worship by choosing hymns appropriate for each section. Congregational hymns and songs can be divided into two broad functional categories: vertical and horizontal.

A vertical hymn is sung in praise to God or of God's attributes. "Praise to the Lord, the Almighty the King of Creation" (written by Joachim Neander) is a classic example of a vertical hymn. "Shout to the Lord All the Earth Let Us Sing" (written by Darlene Zschech) is a contemporary example of a vertical praise song.

Vertical songs and hymns of praise should be placed at the entrance of worship—the Gathering and Praising section—and anywhere else where the congregation is praising and affirming the nature of God.

Horizontal songs are sung by worshipers to each other about their experience with God. These songs offer personal testimonies about what God has done for us. "Amazing Grace" (written by John Newton) is an example of a horizontal song. It should be placed in worship anywhere there is a liturgical need

The Reformation brought into existence a new Church, a new liturgical service, and many new musical practices. Luther modified the Mass and changed it from a liturgy sung by the choir and priests exclusively to a vehicle of congregational worship that included all believers. Martin Luther viewed music as having powers to repulse evil and to glorify God at the same time.

Charles K. Moss,
"The Musical Reforms of Luther"

to give testimony to the power of God's grace in our lives. It is not a song of praise.

Other congregational songs or canticles may serve a particular liturgical need—for example, a communion song, a baptismal song, an offertory or benediction response. Liturgical songs may be either horizontal or vertical in their orientation to God and others. Many hymnals have special sections for this type of service or liturgical music.

These might sound like trivial pursuits. However, if worship is understood as an unfolding drama, then the sequential nature of our musical choices can contribute a great deal to the worshiper's experience.

3. Plan to expand your congregation's repertoire of church music. The most basic goal of congregational music is to provide an avenue whereby worshipers can open their hearts to God and to one another. It is nearly impossible to choose something that will be helpful to everyone at the same time. By their very nature, congregational songs and hymns reflect culture, religious traditions, musical style, language groups, and personal taste. In order to represent an expansive view of God's people and at the same time serve a particular congregation, a strategic approach to congregational singing is necessary. Develop a "landscape" of music to offer the congregation over a year's time.

Remember, there is a season for everything under heaven. There is a time to be pastoral with your musical selections and a time to be prophetic and challenging. Rituals that mark life's transition—funerals, weddings, christenings or baby dedications, retirement celebrations, and baptisms—are examples of occasions when traditional and familiar music is best.

Weekly worship, however, is intended to comfort and to challenge. This is where variety is most appropriate. The chapter called "The Modulating Congregation" deals specifically about handling tension in this area. For now, let us simply affirm that if you are balanced in your approach and faithful to a strategic plan, be firm and take heart. In the long run, your congregation will be grateful.

4. Add movement to congregational singing. When young children want to be held by a parent, they usually raise their arms. It's a childlike gesture of trust and longing. Raising a hand or extending an arm heavenward to God while singing a praise song can be a freeing, heart-opening experience for adults. Teaching your congregation a "sacred gesture" that includes opening the palms and extending the arms can give permission to everyone to express themselves in physical acts of worship.

For example, you might choose an appropriately worshipful praise song with an "Alleluia." Invite the congregation to make the sacred action together during the "Alleluia" section. Always give clear, specific instructions and rehearse the congregation before worship.

5. Surround the congregation with the choir. This can be done most easily at the beginning or at the end of worship. If you're teaching a new song of praise, have the choir process in and surround the congregation. If the new song is a response to the benediction, the choir can easily recess before the singing and surround the congregation on their way out. Do this occasionally throughout the year.

It will connect your congregation to the choir and will give them needed support for learning new songs.

6. Raise the congregation's awareness of the song's message and intent. Print historical notes in each week's bulletin for one of the day's hymns. If you are reluctant to summarize these stories on your own, Austin C. Lovelace has created a good resource published by GIA Publications, Inc. of Chicago called "Hymn Notes for Church Bulletins" for this purpose. These concise paragraphs will deepen your congregation's appreciation for what they are singing.

7. Create hymn supplements with song texts written by your church members. When pianist and songwriter Ken Medema visited our church, he led us in the singing of "Amazing Grace" and then asked someone present to share his or her own story of God's grace. One of the participants told a heart-wrenching story of her daughter's suicide attempt. Ken listened carefully to the story, sat quietly for a moment, and again played "Amazing Grace." This time he sang these words: "We almost lost the one we loved to demons of the mind. But friends be close and God be praised, we'll leave the past behind." Ken said, "Imagine worship where, in addition to singing the stories of past generations, a congregation sings the testimonies of its own members."

Offer poetry-writing workshops for your members to turn their personal stories into metric form for available hymn tunes.

8. Expand your congregation's awareness of church music. Because most congregations today have members from many denominational backgrounds, it is impossible to find one hymnal to satisfy their needs and accomplish your goals. Through copyright licensing services, worship leaders can choose from many songbooks and hymnals integrating a variety of styles into worship. By paying a yearly fee (determined by a sliding scale based on church membership), a church may reproduce the lyrics of hymns and songs, either by inserting them directly into the printed bulletin or by projecting them each week on overhead transparencies or via PowerPoint presentations. This will make worship "user friendly" as congregational

Worship
A Quaker Meeting, a Pontifical High Mass, the Family Service at First Presbyterian, a Holy Roller Happening—unless there is an element of joy and foolishness in the proceedings, the time would be better spent doing something useful.

Frederick Buechner, Wishful Thinking, 98.

singing becomes more accessible to visitors. This printed music can easily be enlarged for visually impaired worshipers.

9. Offer church retreats to focus on music and the spiritual journey. A weekend retreat focused on the power of music in the spiritual life would enhance your congregation's awareness of each other's spiritual history. By understanding unique associations between specific songs and spiritual transformation, members will begin to respect the power of particular music in the lives of others. Over time, this respect will change a congregation's attitude toward music in worship.

10. Exchange choirs often with churches of different ethnic and cultural backgrounds. Exposing your congregation to other cultural styles of praise will allow them to expand their definition of "praise and worship." Since we all think "my way is the right way," the fish tank in which we live stays small. Experiencing the genuine and authentic praise methods of others will begin to expand the size of our life aquarium. We may find that other styles can eventually become authentic for us as well.

11. Offer open choir seasons. Making a long-term commitment to the rigors of church choir rehearsals and presentations is impossible for some church members. Those who could make a short-term commitment would benefit from seasonal participation. Open your choir to members and visitors during the seasons of Advent, Lent, and other appropriate times. Offer a two-tiered commitment such as weekly worship participation plus the special seasonal program on the one hand, and weekly worship or the seasonal program on the other. By arranging the rehearsals so that weekly anthems are rehearsed during the first half and the music for your special program is rehearsed during the last half, singers can choose their level of participation. Options and choices will increase congregational participation in a church's music program.

12. Offer an opportunity to sing well-known works. For years, I have conducted the "Hallelujah Chorus" from Handel's Messiah as a benediction on Easter Sunday. Before beginning the hymn of invitation, invite anyone who would like to sing the "Chorus" with the choir to come forward during the hymn. Music should be placed in a convenient location to be picked up as they move into the choir loft. A variation of this would be to invite the entire assembly to sing the "Hallelujah Chorus" together. (This could work with any piece of well-known choral music.)

Chapter 5

Praying

*That part of the service
which we call response —
whether formal prayer, confession of faith,
hymns or other musical forms —
is all in reality prayer.*

John E. Skoglund, Worship in the Free Churches, 79

PRAYER IS COMMUNICATION WITH GOD. PRAYER
in worship involves spoken and sung prayers as well as silent
prayers. Praying together as God's gathered people is different
from praying alone. Praying together requires thoughtful preparation. Each worship prayer has a unique function, but whatever the
function, always direct your prayers to God. Praying is not a veiled
excuse to preach, make announcements, or offer theological dog-
ma. The following descriptions and suggestions will guide you.

Types of Prayer in the Worship Service
1. The Invocation. From the Latin *invocatis, invocation* means "the
act or process of asking for support, assistance or blessing." In worship the invocation calls upon God to be present to the worshiping
community. It should be short and focused on our need for God.

2. The Prayer of Confession. The prayer of confession offers us the opportunity to be honest with ourselves and with God. During this prayer we present to God those things for which we are genuinely sorry and ask God's forgiveness. A prayer of assurance should be included so that worshipers can, with confidence, receive God's loving forgiveness.

3. The Pastoral Prayer. This prayer is offered by a worship leader and grows out of timely concerns or joys that have arisen in the world, our city, because of sickness or death in the church membership, or due to other concerns and celebrations. Worship leaders should be glad to know about these needs before worship so that they may be included in this prayer time.

One way to create variety in the pastoral prayer is to offer "open-ended" sections of the prayer. For example, ask for God's strength to be with those who are sick and then invite people to respond by announcing the names of their sick loved ones out loud. Another way to create variety is to divide the pastoral prayer into sections such as the world, the community, and the church family. Between each section, sing a congregational antiphon. One example, from the Taizé community, is "Give to us/them your peace, O Jesus Christ."

You might further involve the congregation in the pastoral prayer by implementing one of the following ideas.

❖ **Messages of encouragement.** Create a postcard to be placed in the pew rack so that members can write a message of encouragement to someone mentioned in the pastoral prayer or to someone else God brings to mind. Have them put the person's full name on the card and place it in the offering plate to be addressed and mailed by the church office.

❖ **An altar call.** Invite those who wish to do so to move forward to the front altar or railing prior to the pastoral prayer. Ask members of the congregation to call out the names of those family, friends, and coworkers who need prayer. The pastoral prayer should follow.

4. The Silent Prayer. In addition to being attentive to spoken prayers, silent reflection provides an opportunity to encounter God and enrich the worship experience. Listening to God together in silence is surprisingly meaningful. Rather than isolating worshipers, praying silently together as a community draws us closer. Just as we move from awkward to comfortable silence in our mature human relationships, so it is with God. The more time we spend in silence, the more comfortable it becomes. Some suggestions for silence follow.

❖ **Focus on your breath.** Breath is our most basic gift of life. Inhalation brings a constant flow of life-giving oxygen into our bodies. In the Old Testament, the Hebrew word for "breath" is also translated "spirit." In the New Testament, the Greek word for "air" is also used for "spirit." Both words suggest our breathing to be a divine gift.

   Direction: Focus your awareness on your breathing. As you breathe in, say to yourself, "I am breathing in … thank you for life." As you breathe out, say to yourself, "I am breathing out … receive my living."

❖ **Slowly repeat a passage of Scripture.** Focusing on one short passage of Scripture by repeating it many times allows the worshiper to discover something that might be missed in a quick, one-time reading.

   Direction: Softly repeat, "Create in me a clean heart, O God" or "The Lord is my light, whom shall I fear?" or a similar passage of assurance and affirmation.

❖ **Create positive imagination.** Thoughts are powerful. The wisdom traditions of the world's religions would affirm this truth: "Right thoughts lead to right attitudes which lead to right action." Use the power of imagination to create positive thoughts about another. Offer those thoughts to God. Perhaps your actions will become the answer to your own prayer.

   Direction: Think of someone who needs prayer. Envision that person with the light of Christ encircling his or her life.

Imagination

Like the observatory needs the telescope, the soul needs the imagination. Without an imagination, the soul would have no way of communicating with us, no way to pull our attention to its needs, no way to tell us how deeply we are connected to God.

Jane E. Vennard,
Praying with Body and Soul, 75

❖ **Pray the images that come to you.** Positive meditation can easily slip into negative rumination. Concentrating on your thoughts with awareness will avoid this difficulty.

Direction: Allow your thoughts to arise naturally and without structure. Pray with each thought or image. If an image disturbs you, ask for God's peace. If an image brings you joy, offer that joy to God in thanksgiving.

5. The Lord's Prayer. Time and tradition have proven the profound, abiding meaning of the Lord's Prayer, but as with many time-honored traditions, frequent repetition can render even this powerful part of the Christian liturgy dull and hollow of meaning. Introduce movement or song to enhance your congregation's repetition of the prayer.

❖ Add movement.

Say: Our Father which art in heaven

Direction: (hands rise up and meet over head)

Say: Hallowed be thy name

Direction: (folded hands come down in front of chest)

Say: Thy kingdom come

Direction: (left hand sweeps out in a gathering motion)

Say: Thy will be done

Direction: (right hand sweeps out in a gathering motion)

Say: On earth

Direction: (hands palm down in front sweep a circle, like smoothing out sand)

Say: As it is in heaven

Direction: (palms turned up, straight out in front as if heaven is there)

Say: Give us this day our daily bread

Direction: (cupped hands, fingers in between each other, come together in front of stomach)

Say: And forgive us our sin

Direction: (arms cross across chest)

Say: As we forgive those who sin against us

Direction: (hands reach out to person on either side)

Say: And lead us not into temptation

Direction: (arms cross in front of face, as though chained)

Say: But deliver us from evil

Direction: (arms break out, as if breaking chains)

Say: For thine is the kingdom

Direction: (arms straight out in front)

Say: And the power

Direction: (arms at right angles, fist in air in show of power)

Say: And the glory, forever

Direction: (hands, fingers explode out and upward)

Say: Amen

Direction: (bowed head, hands come back together in front of chest)

❖ **Add music.** Teach your congregation one of the many musical settings of the Lord's Prayer. On each Sunday of a season of the church year or for a month, ask the congregation to respond to the pastoral prayer by singing the Lord's Prayer.

6. The Sign of the Cross. Making the sign of the cross is a powerful symbol of our connection with Christ and Christ's solidarity with us. If you are not in a worshiping tradition that uses the sign of the cross, you may find it helpful. If you are familiar with this sign, use a variation to add depth to its meaning.

- ❖ **Orthodox sign.** Using your right hand, touch forehead, then diaphragm, then right shoulder and left shoulder.
- ❖ **Roman Catholic sign.** Using your right hand, touch your forehead, then diaphragm, then left shoulder and right shoulder.
- ❖ **Celtic sign.** Two hands together make the sign to the forehead, the diaphragm, and then each hand, separately and simultaneously, touches its own shoulder (right hand touches right shoulder; left touches left) before joining together over the heart to finish (Dara Molloy, "Creative Worship in the Celtic Tradition," in *Celtic Threads, 116).*

These signs could be used anytime in worship when you want to honor Christ, to remember your commitment to Christ's way, or to add emphasis to what is happening.

7. Prayers for the Congregation, by the Congregation. Ask your congregation to write prayers for worship and begin a congregational prayer book. This book, arranged by theme, could be used as a worship leadership resource. Praying these prayers in worship will help the congregation feel involved in the preparation and act of corporate worship.

Movement 2

Encountering

UNLESS YOU'VE CHOSEN TO LIVE AS A HERMIT, you do not live your life alone. In our fast-paced world, a hermitage might be something we long for but will not be our daily experience. Instead, our lives are defined by a series of encounters and interactions.

All day we are actively communicating—receiving and sending information through our senses: a political discussion with a coworker, a joke at the check-out stand, a meeting at which important decisions are made, a quick back-and-forth with our children, a conversation with a friend. Our lives are filled with random, often haphazard encounters. Some are meaningful, some painful, but all too often they are hurried.

Encountering the Word

By means of Scripture, Sermon and Sacrament, the living Word of God in the person of Jesus Christ becomes contemporary to the worshiping congregation.

John Skoglund,
Worship in the Free Churches, 58.

As people of faith, we have the opportunity to meet with God each week in worship, not as a random act of devotion but as an intentional encounter with the Creator of the universe. In this context, communication needs to be thoughtfully and authentically given and received.

However, authentic communication is always open to the unexpected, to surprise. This is the nature of anything truly alive. Is this true of our worship? When the gathered people of God open their senses to the written, spoken and living Word, does our worship service allow that Word to take them by surprise? If they were hearing God's Word as if for the first time, wouldn't their hearts genuinely burn within them?

When a congregational encounter with the Word creates hearts open and burning, it becomes the encounter of life. Active worshipers expect that the Word offered to them will be alive so it can take root in their souls. This is what all worshipers anticipate and long for.

Seen in this way, the encounter with the Word in worship becomes the container for all our encounters throughout the week. Each day is an opportunity to put new flesh on that Word. Each moment of the day is a gift to be gently and lovingly opened and enjoyed. Such an expansive view of the encounters in our lives transforms our living and our worship and gives us deeper meaning and genuine satisfaction.

Chapter 6

Reading

The reading [of Scripture] itself
ought to be an act of worship.

Andrew W. Blackwood
The Fine Art of Public Worship, *135*

THERE ARE A VARIETY OF CREATIVE WAYS TO READ
Scripture in the context of worship. When considering more creative options, the most important principles to keep in mind are to present Scripture clearly, articulately, and appropriately.

Clarity
Creativity should never obscure clarity. For example, if a puppet reads the Scripture on Children's Sunday, but the microphone isn't well-placed or the sound technician doesn't have the cue, the congregation will experience creativity but will not hear the word. Creativity must be rehearsed carefully and then delivered in a competent way that opens hearts rather than closing minds.

Articulation
Not everyone cooks well; this doesn't make them inadequate people, it only means they have not yet acquired a particular skill. In the

same way, not everyone reads well. Public reading and speaking is an art form to be taken seriously. When a passage of Scripture is read by someone who has rehearsed the reading and somehow gotten "behind" and "inside" the meaning of the words, those listening will be moved to deeper awareness or to greater service. Scripture poorly delivered carries with it the risk of reducing the encounter with the living God to another random blip on the screen of our weekly experience or, even worse, to a source of irritation.

Appropriateness

Appropriateness in worship flows directly from how well the church leaders know and understand each individual church member—not only their dislikes and prejudices, but more importantly their openness and appreciation of creativity. You may be surprised, as I have been, at many people's high degree of openness and receptivity to innovative Scripture reading. Knowing what will lead your congregation to new depths and what will make them afraid to come to worship is a fine line that can only be walked by one who knows the people who regularly attend the church.

Suggestions to Improve Scripture Reading

1. Read more Scripture in worship, not less. For the gathered people of God, especially in the Protestant tradition, Scripture reading is the basis of our encounter with God. The lectionary usually provides four texts for worship each week: an Old Testament reading, a psalm, a Gospel, and an epistle. Each of these types of Scripture has a different intent, style, and impact. If you do not use the lectionary, find a way to read a selection from all of these kinds of Scripture each week in worship.

2. Allow silence after the Scripture is read. A profound gift to be given in worship is silence. In a world of constant noise and sensory bombardment, allowing people to rest in the words they have just heard restores and transforms the congregation. However, because our world is so noisy, many people don't know how to use silence and only feel uncomfortable with it.

Following the reading of the Gospel, invite the congregation to one minute of silent reflection. Without filling the silence with words, guide them by suggesting they replay the message of the selection, repeat a significant word or phrase from the Scripture, or wait in quiet for an inspiration or thought to rise up within them. As people become accustomed to silent reflection, you may want to increase the silent period.

Before doing this with the entire congregation, consider trying it with a small group. Ask everyone to close their eyes, quiet their mind and focus their attention on the moment at hand. After announcing that there will be five minutes of silence following the reading, ask the reader to read through the Beatitudes from Matthew 5. At the end of the silence, invite everyone to pray the Lord's Prayer together. When eyes are open, ask for a response from their listening. The collective wisdom and insight will be an encouragement to all.

3. Develop a lay readers school. Throughout church history, Scripture reading in worship has belonged to lay readers. Professional clergy have too often taken this gift away from the laity. Many people in your congregation are excellent oral interpreters. If Scripture readings are chosen ahead of time, these readers could meet once a month with a teacher and practice the fine art of reading in public, giving attention to voice projection, emphasis, changes in loudness and timbre, etc. The teacher could be a drama coach, amateur actor or former actor, or a naturally gifted lay reader from your congregation.

Vary men and women's voices throughout the service, and vary ages, races, and accents as well. Doing so will give people an expansive view of God. If the biblical passage is a story with characters, different voices can be used for each character in a semi-dramatic or "readers' theater" performance.

4. Arrange a visit from a prophet. Another dramatic way for a congregation to experience an encounter with prophetic words in Scripture is hearing from that prophet "in person." Create the prophet's costume for one of your dramatic readers, affix the prophetic Scripture passage into a scroll, and maybe even give the reader a dramatic entrance such as from the back of the church. Allow the congregation to get a feel for "a voice crying in the wilderness." For example, if your congregation celebrates the Advent season, the church could experience a visit from the prophet Isaiah on the first Sunday of Advent.

5. Read responsively or antiphonally. Responsive readings are a valuable way to involve the entire congregation in the experience of reading Scripture. In this setting, an individual reader and the group take turns reading a Scripture text verse-by-verse. Different sections of the congregation—for example the right and left sides or choir and congregation—can also read verses back and forth to each other.

Antiphonal readings are slightly different; one of the groups or an individual repeats a single phrase or sentence (called the "antiphon") between verses of the Scripture passage. This practice is commonly done with the psalms but can be used for a variety of texts. For example, the congregation may read a psalm and an individual reader would say, "The steadfast love of the Lord never ceases" between each verse.

One variation is to have a person or the choir sing the antiphon. Singing the antiphon is an effective way to fix the truth of what's being said in the worshiper's mind. Whether you use a bulletin insert, large screens with PowerPoint or an overhead projector, prepare the responsive reading or the antiphon in a way that clearly communicates your intent to all involved.

6. Sing one of the readings as an anthem. Many passages of Scripture have been beautifully set as anthems. As the choir's contribution to worship that day, ask them to sing the Scripture reading, allowing a moment of silence to follow. Your director of music will appreciate knowing the plan well in advance. You might invest in computer software that sorts hymns and anthems by Scripture reference (available in many music and Christian book stores). Another important resource for church musicians is *Creator Magazine* which began in 1978. They describe themselves as the first multi-denominational publication about music ministry. Their website is: www.creatormagazine.com.

7. Sign the Scripture reading even if you have no hearing impaired members. Of course, if you have hearing impaired members, you're doing this already. For those who do not understand sign language, the interpretive movement of the signs will reinforce what they are hearing through a different sensory avenue.

8. Create a short antiphon and teach the sign language for it to the congregation. For example, if the prayer "The Lord Is My Strength and Song" fits into the Scripture reading as an antiphonal affirmation, have the congregation sign those words each time it is said or sung. The last time the antiphon is said, use only hand signs with no spoken words. Your congregation can take that gift home with them and sign that prayer to each other when words seem inadequate.

9. Re-create an important event on a special Sunday of the church year. This suggestion works extremely well on Pentecost Sunday. Find people who read well in another language and ask them to provide the text for Acts 2 in their language. Because of the national backgrounds of the people in my congregation, I've used English, Spanish, Swedish, Tamal, and Kituba. If you're blessed to have people who speak multiple languages in your congregation, count those blessings! The primary reader uses the dominant language of your congregation (in the example below, I'm assuming an English-speaking congregation with the foreign language readers I had available to me). When this reading is carefully rehearsed and artistically directed, it has a profound effect.

English: Acts 2:1
Spanish: Acts 2:1
English: Acts 2:2

Swedish: Acts 2:2
English: Acts 2:3
Tamal: Acts 2: 3
English: Acts 2:4
Kituba: Acts 2:4
English: Acts 2:6
All readers in their own language at the same time: Acts 2:6
(Momentary pause)
English: Acts 2:37-38
English and Spanish: Acts 2:38 *(starting with "Repent")*
English, Spanish, and Tamal: Repeat Acts 2:38
        (starting again with "Repent")
English, Spanish, Tamal, and Kituba: Repeat Acts 2:38
        (starting again with "Repent")
(At this point all readers are reading the last portion of verse 38, at the same time, in a loud voice, each in his or her own language. Repeating the verse increases the dramatic effect.)
(Momentary pause)
English: Acts 2:42 *(reflectively)*

10. If you have technology, use it. If you have the capability to effectively use video technology in your sanctuary, there are many excellent resources available to you. One I can recommend is The Genesis Project, creators of the Media Bible. Their website is: www.genesisnewmediabible.com, and they describe their work in the following way: "The Genesis Project, Inc. is an international group of Christian and Jewish archaeologists, historians and biblical scholars, educators, filmmakers, and creative artists who joined together to help churchmen and educators, institutions and individuals transmit the ethics, ideas, and faith of the Bible in an age dominated by electronic media."

Painstakingly researched and carefully crafted, this series of videos portrays biblical characters reading from the Gospel of Luke in Hebrew and Aramaic as well as English. These subtitled videos would add a sense of drama and authenticity to the reading of the Word in worship.

11. Stand or kneel for the lesson. Invite your congregation to stand or kneel for the reading of the Scripture lesson. By symbolizing respect and giving special attention through the posturing of your body, you will find that the reading of the Scripture takes on new emphasis and importance as a high point in worship.

Chapter 7

The Preaching Moment

Preaching ... has a double stubbornness:
it is stubbornly the same,
and it is stubbornly there.

Clyde E. Fant, Preaching for Today, 1

THE DOVE IDEA WAS THE MOST CREATIVE THING
to come into his mind for quite some time. Pastor Kinney had been
looking forward to this Sunday for weeks. It was the "Baptism of
Our Lord," and this was his dramatic moment.

As he reluctantly helped the custodian put Christmas decora-
tions away, the idea had come to him with an unexpected swoosh
and bang! No one knew about that trap door in the ceiling until
all his weight was on it. With one leg dangling into the sanctuary
and the custodian making a rescue attempt, the rather embarrassed
pastor experienced his imaginative wheels turning. Creativity often
comes at strange moments of weakness.

He had been wondering how to make re-enactment come to
life. Fortunately, the Gospel text for the day read like a script,
"The heavens opened and the Holy Spirit descended as a dove!"
Perfect. Tommy Wilson seemed to be the most likely middle-
schooler to climb into the attic. Pastor Kinney quietly rented the

dove and the cage from a local bird shop, and the scene was set.

Saturday's rehearsal went surprisingly well. Tommy ascended easily up the back passage and found his way to the now familiar trap door. Five minutes into the practice sermon, at just the right dramatic moment, the pastor lifted his gaze toward heaven and bellowed the cue, "and the Holy Spirit descended as a dove." Like a pro, Tommy tossed that startled bird down into the chancel.

Wings flapping, feathers flying, the pure white and sudden action of that moment took even Pastor Kinney by surprise. "Wow, this is great!" he whispered, pleased that the scraping and bruising that had given birth to his idea a few weeks ago now seemed worth it. It took an hour to coax the dove back into the cage from the rafters of the sanctuary, but that was to be expected, a small price to pay for this kind of realism. He swore Tommy to secrecy and put the dove in the attic for the night.

The big day finally arrived. The scheduled baptisms assured him of a good crowd. Pastor Kinney's self-confidence was evident as he shunned his black robe with white stole for the all white vestment option on this special Sunday. Following a long processional, the anthem, three different Scripture readings, and after the christening during which he walked two dripping babies through an adoring congregation, he finally stepped into the pulpit with a gleam in his eye. During the baptisms, Tommy had moved into place.

The pastor began what he was certain would be one of the most memorable sermons he'd ever preached. As the well-rehearsed text appeared on his manuscript, he threw back his head and, with a roar the likes of which his congregation hadn't heard before, he delivered the words he'd been waiting to say, "and the Holy Spirit descended as a dove!" The silence was deafening. Assuming Tommy wasn't ready, he shrugged it off and said with renewed vigor, "and the Holy Spirit descended as a dove!" Still, nothing happened. This time, he was getting nervous and spoke what sounded more like a plea, "and the Holy Spirit descended as a dove." The trap door opened and a sheepish voice floated down through the rafters, "The cat ate the Holy Spirit! You want me to throw the cat down?"

Background

Preaching is an awesome responsibility and a privilege. Discerning the meaning of a text and applying that meaning to life can be one of the most fulfilling parts of ministry. However, preaching can also be one of the deadliest parts of worship.

In the flow of worship, an imaginative, well crafted, skillfully delivered sermon moves the worshiper into a deeper encounter with God and invites a variety of responses. An image-laden, personal message has staying power and becomes a resource for our living. At its best, preaching is a sacrament, a holy and sacred action filled with evocative meaning. At its worst, sermonizing becomes a pothole on the journey of worship, sometimes large enough to swallow entire sections of the sanctuary.

By definition, preaching has everything to do with communicating a message or an idea. Creative preaching ideas can become vehicles for transferring wisdom and grace to the listener, or they can act as filters that cloud and distort the meaning. Because of the power and status given to the "preaching moment" especially in reformation traditions, creativity must be carefully and thoughtfully applied to the sermon.

Suggestions for Making Preaching More Effective

1. Remember that less is often more. Unless there are no other opportunities for your church members to study the Bible, the sermon should not be a Bible study. A sermon should be inspirational. In a day of decreasing attention spans, a sermon that goes beyond twenty minutes is in danger of losing its effectiveness for most people. Focus on one central controlling idea.

2. Move away from the pulpit. Pulpits are symbols of dignity, respect and power. For some listeners, sermons from the pulpit carry those attributes. Pulpits can also be barriers standing between the spoken Word and the otherwise receptive worshiper. If a preacher has a gift for memorization or is confident with an extemporaneous style, moving away from the pulpit can create an atmosphere of openness and accessibility.

3. Use an evocative image to help convey meaning. The saying "a picture is worth a thousand words" is taken seriously by those teaching English as a second language. For them, a picture is the means by which they teach meaning. I once handed out to each worshiper a color photograph of a statue in the courtyard of the Chester Cathedral in England. This stunning image of Jesus and the woman at the well served as a visual representation of a powerful encounter with Christ and reinforced the message of the sermon. For some, that photo became a permanent reminder in their home or office.

4. Preach dialogically. Preaching with someone else is an effective way to add variety. Experiment with several formats. These could include a question/answer interview, a dramatic presentation in which each preacher represents a character in the biblical story for the day, or one person offering textual background while another offers interpretation and inspiration. Alternating men and women's voices and utilizing different accents and languages, especially for the voice of God, is important and expansive.

5. Try a monologue. Dressing in character and delivering a sermon from the perspective of a biblical personality is imaginative and enjoyable. There are often skilled actors and writers in the congregation. Take advantage of those gifts by encouraging them to be "in the spotlight."

6. Use art and sculpture as illustrations. Many encounters with Christ and other spiritual themes have been depicted through famous paintings. Displayed electronically or as a bulletin insert, these works can provide a backdrop for character and theme development in the sermon. Offer silent reflection and ask worshipers to identify with someone in the painting.

7. Include the choir or congregational singing. An anthem might provide just the right illustration to enhance an idea or visual image. Have the choir or the congregation sing at planned intervals throughout the sermon.

8. Pay attention to your nonverbal cues. The power of nonverbal communication embodied in the preacher should be taken seriously. It includes the use of your body (face, eyes and mouth, hands, head, limbs, and trunk), eye contact, gestures, appearance, clothing, the environment (time and physical characteristics), and the use of space. Videotape yourself preaching in the sanctuary. Gather your worship team. After giving them paper and pencil, turn the sound down on the monitor and watch your sermon together. Make sure they cannot hear a word you say. During and after the sermon, ask them to write down the impressions they gained from simply watching your body language. You'll be enlightened and amazed. Do this often and it will change the way you think about the nonverbal world of communication.

9. Offer a sermon-feedback series on Sunday evenings. If you preach a series of sermons on one topic, ask the congregation to meet with you for a "fireside chat" on those Sunday evenings to answer their questions and delve deeper into the meaning of the

---

Nonverbal Communication
The preacher needs to become aware of the world of the nonverbal. In theological education the emphasis is on the power of verbal language. It is a misplaced emphasis, given the reality of the Incarnation. The embodiment of the Word in human body language invites each minister of the Word to explore the power of nonverbal language.

Myron Chartier, Preaching as Communication, 92

> *The Power of Stories*
> *It is largely our failure to draw the proper analogies which has dulled the cutting edge of the gospel and which has turned the radical message of the New Age in Christ into Sunday morning "helpful hints for hurtful habits" (as Paul Scherer has phrased it). . . . retell the biblical story in vivid and imaginative language and let [your] people enter into it.*
>
> *Elizabeth Achtemeier,* Creative Preaching, 71

morning's text. View this as an opportunity to listen to the wisdom of the members of your congregation as they dialogue with you and with Scripture. Serve refreshments and make it a relaxed, inviting time of interaction.

10. Take a storytelling class. It has been said, "the closest distance between two people is a story." Storytelling is a thriving art in cultures that value the oral tradition. Narrative artistry is a skill and can be learned. Call the local "folk club" or adult learning center in your city and ask about storytelling classes or workshops. People may forget the points of your sermon but they will not forget a well-told story.

Movement 3
Responding

We've all heard the familiar words attributed to Benjamin Franklin, "There are two certainties in life—death and taxes." Growing up on the plains of Kansas, I learned another certainty. "The wind blows every day." Whenever I visited my cousins in Pennsylvania I wondered what happened to the wind. Then we returned to Kansas and I realized nothing happened to the wind. It was blowing the entire time I was gone.

There is an amazing constancy in the natural world. Clouds form. Rain comes. Birds sing. The sun shines (even if we don't see it). The gifts of nature are all around us. We receive a gift every time we breathe. We

> By calling us beyond what we are or think we can be, whether in relation to ourselves or others, God surprises us with a sense of the potential of our own fuller humanity, our being in the very image of God.
>
> Jean M. Blomquist, "Daily Dancing with the Holy One," in Weavings, 10

don't request or deny the gifts of the natural world. They just come.

It is that "givenness" all around us that reminds us of God's grace. Whether we want it or not, grace is present to us. Poet Coleman Barks tells the story of growing up in rural Tennessee where, as a child, he was in love with the beauty of the natural world. He describes a day when a rainbow formed over a nearby hill. Barely able to catch his breath, he rolled on the floor with his arms around himself. When his mother asked him what his problem was, he said, "I've just got that full feeling again."

The "givenness" of God creates a full feeling in those who receive it. In theological language, we label God's presence "revelation." I prefer the term "givenness" because for me that word is evocative. The "givenness" of God through the incarnation of Christ, through the created order, through humanity, through mighty acts recorded in the Bible coax me to respond, not with a patterned response—a formula by which my response can be judged—rather, I respond freely with all the wisdom and uniqueness of my life's experiences.

In some ways, everything we do in worship could be described as our grateful response to the "givenness" of God. Receive the goodness and grace of God, and free yourself to respond from a grateful heart.

Chapter 8

Communion

*A desire for communion has been
part of you since you were born.*

Henri J. M. Nouwen
The Inner Voice of Love, 95

AS A YOUNG PERSON IN WORSHIP, I USED TO
look forward to the first Sunday of the month when our church
celebrated the Lord's table. Mostly, I was hungry because it was
almost noon and I'd been at church all morning. Finally, at the end
of worship, around came the bread and the juice. (We always
called it the cup. Jesus would have "taken the cup"; he would never have "taken the juice.") No matter how good I thought it was
going to be, I was never satisfied. That tiny cup and that little wafer
barely made a dent in my growling stomach.

Since, in our tradition, all who received the cup waited for
everyone to get theirs, I sat and stared into it until it was time to
partake. If I held the cup just right, I could catch the lights of the
sanctuary on the surface of the juice. The reflection of those lights
seemed to form in the shape of a star. Then the words of institution were pronounced and I gulped it down, star and all.

That star later became a symbol for me. It helped me realize there was more than juice in that cup. What was it? Now, in my forties, I still ask that question. Whatever the answer, it doesn't help my growling stomach, but it nourishes my soul.

The Lord's Supper, no matter how often we celebrate it, is the act of communing with Christ. As we gather around the broken body of Jesus, the risen Christ is in our midst. It is our unity with Christ that makes the Lord's Supper more than a memorial meal. More than bringing to mind and honoring the events of the past, Communion provides an opportunity for mystery in worship. Christ, the bread of life, in a way that is beyond our reasoning, becomes our nourishment. Christ's birth, death, and resurrection—and ours—come together in this act of faith.

This coming together of the past, the present, and the future is the meaning of symbolism. The word symbol literally means "to throw together." As symbols, the elements of the Lord's table are an extraordinary representation of ordinary food. Bread is the basic food of most cultures of the world. In many cultures wine is also a basic food. Yet, as was his habit, Jesus took the everyday "stuff" of life and "threw it together" in a new way.

Symbols are real, present, in front of us. But symbols also evoke something beyond the reality in front of us; they evoke something unique in each of us. Bread and wine are symbols of Christ—what he did, what he is doing and what he will do. But they are more than that. They represent a longing in us for communion with divine reality.

In the act of Communion, there is nothing we do to make Christ more present than Christ already is. But through the symbols of bread and wine, we can open our lives in new ways to that presence. That is the gift of faith we bring to the Lord's table.

Suggestions for the Communion Service

1. Prepare Communion elements as an act of prayer. Those who prepare the bread and wine for Communion are partners in the process of making something ordinary become extraordinary.

64

Through loving and prayerful preparation, the elements become representations not only of Christ but also of each person who will participate in the Communion service. Their needs, hurts, joys and desires will all come with them to the table of the Lord. All the gifts we bring can come back to us transformed if we present them with open hearts and willing spirits. That openness begins with those who prepare the meal.

2. Consider introducing movement. Worshipers need opportunities to present themselves to God. Many congregations stay seated while Communion is passed to them. This allows them to serve the person next to them while they pass the tray. While serving each other has its own symbolic meaning reflecting the congregation's communion with each other through their communion with Jesus, coming forward has a different and equally valuable symbolism. It is a more deliberate act of worship that expresses each Christian's desire and willingness to present his or herself to God. Encourage the congregation to walk forward to receive the bread and cup and, in this way, present themselves to Christ.

3. Change the elements. Instead of a wafer and individual cups of juice, use grapes and a variety of colors of bread. The bread will represent the variety of people who participate with us around the world in the act of Communion. The juice of the grape, which ferments into wine, is essentially the life force of the grape—the "blood" of the grape.

4. Invite worshipers to the feast of Christ. Set a long banquet table at the front of the sanctuary representing the marriage feast of the Lamb. For the sake of time, make sure it seats enough people to include all worshipers in no more than five or six seatings. Invite people to come forward in groups to sit at this banquet table. Welcome them to the feast of the Lord and speak the words of institution over each group before that group partakes together.

5. Remember Christ at home. Commemorate Christ's Last Supper around your own table at a dinner party with family and friends. As Christ took the ordinary and made it extraordinary, it is good for us to remember Christ as we eat a meal in our own home surrounded by our own ordinariness. If your church or tradition has strong reservations about lay persons administering the Communion elements, worship leaders can prepare a printed home Communion service for their congregants to use as a guide. This type of on-going celebration of Christ's presence enriches our experience of Communion in worship by making corporate remembrance and table fellowship a part of everyday life.

Chapter 9

Giving

If you wish to be perfect,
go, sell your possessions,
and give the money to the poor,
and you will have treasure in heaven ...

Matthew 19:21, NRSV

THERE IS A TREND IN CHURCHES TODAY TO ELIMinate the offering from the worship service. The motivation for this decision is attributed to "seeker sensitivity." A seeker has been defined by those advocating this trend as a person who is intelligent, searching for spiritual truth but religiously suspicious. By not asking them to give, so the thinking goes, these seekers will feel less suspicious.

In our day of commercialized religion, I agree that many people are skeptical when it comes to the church. However, in my perspective, deleting the offering from worship is not the answer to their mistrust.

In our day when non-profit organizations have taken advantage of their status, and religious leaders have abused their authority, suspicion and skepticism are society's ways of providing accountability. This is reasonable and necessary. We must remember that a large part of Jesus' mission on earth was to challenge the direction and practice of a misguided religious institution.

When it comes to money and the church, one of my mentors taught me an important piece of strategic wisdom early in my ministry. He said, "when asking for money, always tell people why their money is needed, thank them for giving and tell them how their money was used." This simple formula provides honest communication, gratitude for gifts given and financial accountability. If givers don't like the way money is spent, they will choose not to give. To have religious integrity, we must give them that choice. This strategy will go a long way toward healing religious cynicism.

The Church's Dilemma

Clearly, many people are generous and big hearted. When national or international disasters occur, humanity is seen at its best as states and countries respond with aid and teams of relief workers. The "acute" nature of a disaster makes it possible to define quickly the need and respond with specific and appropriate assistance.

Churches, for the most part, do not have "acute" needs. Keeping the lights on and paying salaries is only acute if you believe in the work and ministry of the church. Religious organizations are "chronic" institutions. They have ongoing, complex financial needs.

My personal life experience gives me compassion for this dilemma. When our son's brain tumor was life threatening, our friends, church and family went into "disaster-relief mode." In a very real way, we could not have coped without them.

After the crisis passed, our needs were less defined, less "acute." The chronic nature of living with disabilities and disappointments made it less possible for our friends to know how to help. Families who live with physical and mental handicaps and chronic medical challenges learn to be more deliberate with their family and friends about their needs.

Because our family and friends "believe in us" and love us, they are happy to help but they have to know the need. That communication is our responsibility.

The Value of Giving

Worshipers will respond to God's invitation to give if they understand the point of their giving. The motivation has to be as large as the God doing the inviting. Giving to the chronic needs of a religious organization is not what God is asking of us.

The dictionary defines money as "a standard piece of [precious metal] stamped by government authority and used as a measure of value." Worship is the attributing of worth to God. Money symbolizes that which we value most. Giving our money to God is an act of worship. A local church is the vehicle for that act of worship and provides the opportunities for service that our giving creates. Providing people the opportunity to give their financial resources as an act of worship distinguishes the local church from other service organizations.

Worship is also our grateful response to the self-giving of God in the person of Jesus Christ. For Christians, a grateful response to God's gift of life calls forth nothing less than that which we most value. In worship, rather than removing the offering, we want to create many ways for people to respond generously.

Suggestions for a Worshipful Offering

1. Provide education for the congregation. Start your education with this formula: first, honest communication; second, gratitude for gifts given; and third, financial accountability.

Honest communication should be inspirational as well as factual. The mission department of the church I recently served was wise and generous in their vision for mission education. They invited missionaries to live among the congregation for a lengthy period of time. These men and women had an expansive effect on the congregation. Through them, church members came to understand mission work around the world. This made it possible for worshipers to see their giving as part of the global work of Christ, not just a maintenance agreement with a local church.

Gratitude for gifts given includes personal visits and notes for specific gifts but also should reflect an interest in people apart from their money. Nothing raises a person's level of cynicism more than hearing from the church only when money is needed. Personal contact between church leaders and the congregation is critically important.

2. Celebrate the gifts given. Financial accountability includes more than making spending records available to people. Certainly, open and accessible accounting of expenses is necessary in the church. But celebration is more important. Church business meetings should be parties of celebration focused on what God is doing in the world through the gifts of a local congregation. Make it a Frank Capra kind of "It's a Wonderful Life" evening where the church, like George Bailey, realizes the world would be a gloomier, darker place without them. The financial integrity of the entire congregation makes the shedding of Christ's light possible on that corner of the world, in that specific place.

3. Always include giving in worship. Many nonprofit organizations make automatic bank withdrawal possible for their donors. This is a streamlined, efficient way to garner financial support. Although charity and love are not exclusive to the church, among nonprofit organizations the church must retain its identity as the body and bride of Christ. Gathering together to worship God is what makes the church unique. The act of giving, as a vital part of worship, should always be included.

4. Invite worshipers to come forward more often. In his book *The Way of the Traveler,* Joseph Dispenza describes a friend who, "when she dreams the dream of travel, ... consciously moves from one spot to another. That is all! She stands in one place in one room of her house and mentally calls that 'home.' Then she walks slowly and carefully into another room—to a spot that she has designated 'the destination.' To complete the [journey] she walks, just as slowly and carefully, back to her original spot" (12). "It is really the simplest thing in the world," Dispenza notes, "and, like most simple things, remarkably meaningful"(11).

Worship is a journey. As worship leaders, providing opportunities for movement, particularly to an offering box in the front of the sanctuary, gives worshipers the important physical experience of moving toward God. A choir anthem or a congregational song about service, giving of one's self, surrender, or commitment to God creates an appropriate setting.

5. Teach children that giving is part of worship. Always make children a part of the invitation to give. Our children each have a banking system that allows them to divide their money into three categories: Invest, Save, and Spend/Give. Called the World of Money Allowance Kit, this bookshelf bank teaches them to make giving part of their financial planning. Bringing their money to worship and placing it in the box or plate teaches them their essential place in the worshiping community. (To obtain these kits for use in your own church school, contact the World of Money at 800-513-3779.)

6. Invite people to bring symbols of their gifts/talents to worship. This invitation could be for a special Sunday in conjunction with a sermon on the topic or it could be a weekly, monthly, or quarterly invitation. The congregation represents all the gifts and talents that make up the body of Christ. In order for the body to function properly, each gift is valuable. Symbols will be as personal and unique as the gift they represent. Invite the congregation to place their symbols on the altar as a sign of their presence in the worshiping community and their work in the body of Christ.

Chapter 10

Baptism

By baptism we were buried with him,
and lay dead, in order that,
as Christ was raised from the dead
in the splendor of [God], so also we might
set our feet upon the new path of life.

Romans 6:4, NEB

AFTER THE BIRTH OF MY CHILDREN, TWO OF THE most fulfilling experiences of my life have been celebrating their new life through baptism. At age twelve, they couldn't articulate the theology I knew about their decision to follow Christ in that act, but they knew what they were doing. My head and heart were ablaze with gratitude and awe.

After eight years of struggling with cancer, enduring sixteen surgeries, and learning to live with disabilities, Brandon stood before his congregation to proclaim to the world that he was going to follow Jesus as a disciple. As I submerged him into the character of Christ, it was almost more than this dad could take.

Brianna followed two years later. Looking into her eyes filled with the pain and courage that marks a cancer sibling, I could see she was making one of the most important decisions of her life. I asked her if she had received Jesus Christ as her Lord and if she would follow him in a lifetime of service. Her answer was "yes," and I baptized her in the name of God the Creator, God the Redeemer, and God the Sustainer. At that moment I felt like Simeon who, after seeing God's salvation at work, could depart in peace.

In keeping with the religious tradition of his day, Jesus practiced a form of ritual washing called the mikveh. This ceremonial cleansing was a symbol of purification and consecration and was a common practice before entering a sacred site or performing a sacred act. Christian baptism gets its inspiration from the mikveh.

Using the baptism of Jesus as our model, we can affirm three things that happened to my children that day and that happen to anyone who stirs those waters. In the scriptural account describing when John the Baptizer baptized Jesus, we can see three distinct affirmations: (1) A voice spoke from the heavens confirming Jesus as God's beloved son; (2) John became Jesus' disciple, and (3) Jesus entered his public ministry. We can see those three affirmations as a metaphor for our lives. In our own baptism we are confirmed as a child of God; we become a follower of Christ; and we begin the ministry to which we have each been called.

In describing the meaning of baptism, Paul, writing to the church in Rome, also used Christ's life as a metaphor for ours. In our baptism, we were buried with Christ and have been raised to newness of life through his resurrection.

Historically, the theologies of baptism have been used to distinguish Christians from one another, to keep us separate and apart. In reality, the act of baptism is what binds us together in the family of God. In 1 Corinthians, the apostle Paul affirmed that there is only one baptism. Therefore, no matter what form baptism takes, through that act of faith, Christians worldwide share equally in the life, death, and resurrection of Christ. Through each baptized person, Christ breaks into our world in one more unique and beautiful way. Celebrating that incarnate reality is a significant part of worship.

Suggestions for Baptismal (and Dedication) Services

1. Baptism is a communal event. It is appropriate for the entire church to support the baptism of others. Candle lighting brings this support to life. As an example, let's say there are five baptismal candidates for one service. Place six candles on the altar or communion table. As a person is baptized, someone they invited who has been a significant in their spiritual journey comes forward and lights one of the candles as a sign of blessing and support. This repeats for each candidate. There will be one candle left unlit. The minister explains that this candle symbolizes those who have yet to make this decision. The body of Christ is not yet complete. There is more room in the family of God.

2. Celebrate those who have been baptized. Offer a churchwide luncheon in honor of those who have been baptized that morning and their families whom they then introduce to the congregation. Give the newly baptized members a gift symbolic of the significance of the day.

3. Dedicate infants and their parents. If your church baptizes only those who make an adult decision to follow Christ, create significant services of dedication for infants and their parents. Committing infants to God's care and offering support to their parents is a significant part of being in a church community. Recognizing infants as belonging to God reminds the congregation of their responsibility in nurturing that child to a point of personal decision.

4. Allow the candidates for baptism to speak. Ask those being baptized to memorize a verse of Scripture that signifies their commitment to Christ, or to share a word of personal testimony. As that person enters the baptistry, ask them to recite that verse for the congregation. This will both express their personal faith and make the Bible an important part of their baptism experience.

5. Ask the congregation to respond. Create a church tradition of sending cards the week following a person's baptism. Cards of congratulations and welcome from many members of the church add significance to the commitments that have been made.

Movement 4

Embracing

Those of us who are strong
and able in the faith need to step in
and lend a hand to those who falter,
and not just do what is most convenient for us.
Strength is for service, not status.
Each one of us needs to look after
the good of the people around us,
asking ourselves, "How can I help?"
That's exactly what Jesus did.
He didn't make it easy for himself
by avoiding people's troubles,
but waded right in and helped out.

Romans 15:1-3, The Message

Chapter 11

Sending

Send us out to proclaim
the reign of your Kingdom.
Send us out to proclaim and to heal.
Send us out with your power and your authority
to overcome and to heal the world.

John Michael Talbot, "Send Us Out"

THROUGH MY YEARS OF PASTORAL MINISTRY, I have had the privilege of participating in and later leading many mission work teams around the world. I count those experiences as some of the most meaningful of my life. Because of the difficulty of the work, the poverty of those we served, and the language barriers between us, most of those tours have humbled me. Upon our return from each trip, I viewed my life and the world around me with new eyes and a new heart.

True humility is risky. Humility is often seen as a penitential state of contrition. But the word *humble* comes from the Latin "humus" meaning fertile soil. This etymology creates a metaphor that expands my vision. A humble person is a nutrient-rich, porous garden of potential.

Rather than focusing us on our own lack of worth or inabilities,

> *"Whoever wishes to be great among you must be your servant . . . even as the Son of Man came not to be served but to serve."*
>
> Matthew 20:26,28, NRSV

true humility opens us to the possibility of new life. Rather than creating oppression, it allows greater expression for our love of God. It is our deep longing to express that love that calls us into the world as servants of Christ.

The churches I've served have been careful to take seriously the work of mission teams. Those teams would never "disappear into mission." The commitment of those who go is too deep for that. A service of blessing and commissioning is the best way to honor their big hearts.

Gathered on the platform in the sanctuary, a group of servants prepares to give their lives to others for two weeks. They need to hear words worthy of their desire to go. The fact that they are doing the right thing for God needs to reverberate with cosmic clarity. "As the Father sends me, so I send you," says Jesus.

With the assured presence of heaven and angels, the congregation holds hands and wraps them in love. They go as representatives of this local body of believers. It is a partnership of service and a pilgrimage of trust.

That is a fitting image for the gathered people of God moving out into the world each week to love and serve. Those who have come together to remember Christ are now willing to be dismembered—to scatter into the workweek with its challenges, frustrations, and joy. They go as the body of Christ in the world, representing the hope, grace, and power of the One whom they follow as disciples.

As a Taizé chant affirms, "Where charity and love are found, there is God." Make it so, people of God!

Suggestions for Cultivating a Spirit of Service

1. Place opportunities for service in the foyer. There are many opportunities to love and serve those in need, and there is no end to the needs. Find service agencies or servant ministries that match your church's core values and place their brochures in the foyer of the church. As you send the congregation into the world, point out those possibilities to the congregation. People need practical suggestions to which they can respond.

2. Organize mission teams often. Your denomination will assist you in finding the right mission for your congregation. If you are not affiliated with a particular group, many parachurch organizations will help you. World Servants is one group with a proven track record. Contact them at: www.worldservants.org or 800-881-2170. Ongoing mission increases a congregation's awareness of the important Christian cycle of worship and service.

3. All service is mission. It's easy to assume that "mission" means speaking a foreign language and going overseas. Mission and ministry are not the domain of professionals. In a broad sense, anyone who serves the human family in the name of Christ is a missionary. When you learn of unique ways your congregants serve others, honor their call to ministry by commissioning them for that service. In that way, all Christians are "ordained to the gospel ministry."

4. Celebrate service with a ministry festival. Many churches schedule their annual business meeting in January. Since January begins the Season of Epiphany, celebrating the appearance of Christ into all the world, this would be a perfect opportunity to celebrate all the ministries of the church. These ministries are "epiphanies of service" in a local congregation. Have every ministry from the altar guild to the nursery represented. As a fund-raiser for their next activity, encourage the youth to provide finger food at a modest cost. Have a party in celebration of service!

5. Hold a foot-washing service. Especially if you are a member of a church tradition that does not practice foot-washing on a regular basis, integrating the act into a worship service can be profoundly moving, for participants and observers alike. The foot washing can be handled in a variety of ways. You might ask two volunteers (in advance) to come forward and wash each other's feet during a regular Sunday service, as an illustration for the congregation.

Alternatively you could hold a separate service that would involve the entire congregation in the act. Church leaders might wash the feet of the members, symbolizing submission to Christ's model of servant leadership. Or, members might wash the feet of their leaders, demonstrating support and affirmation of that leadership. Too, you might have spouses wash each other's feet, or younger adults wash the feet of the elder members of the church. Whichever option you choose or whatever other variations you employ, the service will take on unique significance for your congregation.

6. Encourage your deacons to model servant leadership. I don't mean to pick on the deacons. All leaders in the church are servant leaders.

But deacons, if you have them, carry a specific torch of service. The term *deacon* comes from the New Testament word *diakonia*. *Dia* means "through" and *konos* means "dust" or "dirt." Rather than a position of power, the diaconate is a position of service. Have your deacons model that ministry of service in all they do. Start with regular visitations with your home-bound members.

Chapter 12

Benediction and Response

Deep peace of the running wave to you.
Deep peace of the flowing air to you.
Deep peace of the quiet earth to you.
Deep peace of the shining stars to you.
Deep peace of the gentle night to you.
Moon and stars pour their healing light on you.
Deep peace of the Light of the World to you.
Deep peace to you.

Traditional Celtic blessing

WE'VE ALL HEARD OF FAIR-WEATHER FANS. IF
we're honest with ourselves, at one time or another, we've proba-
bly been one. Fair-weather fans leave the game when it becomes
obvious their team is going to lose. We've all seen it on television.
Shortly after half time, with a lopsided score, the discussions begin.
"We could leave now and beat the traffic." "Let's go home and get
dinner started. We can always watch the game on television in case
it gets close again." Slowly through the third and fourth quarter,
the stadium becomes more and more empty. Without hesitation,
people get up and walk out.

There can be no fair-weather fans in worship. The pews don't begin to empty out half way through just because the choir didn't rehearse the anthem well enough. This is worship. We're here to meet with God.

Leaving worship is a sacred action and an act of faith. When done with renewed courage and hope, walking out of the sanctuary symbolizes our desire to serve and love the world. When done with an open heart, leaving the gathered people of God symbolizes leaving our securities to venture into a sometimes hostile world.

Sacred leave-taking needs to be ritualized and honored as a necessary part of the drama of worship, and those who leave need to be blessed with God's power over their lives.

Suggestions for the Benediction

1. When you send your congregation into the world, look at them. The benediction is most effective when it is said directly to people. Looking into their eyes reminds people to receive the benediction with their eyes open. Since the Latin words bene and diction mean, "good speech," make your benediction an affirmation of something good. Smile and put life into your voice.

2. Revisit a theme from your sermon. In one or two sentences, reframe a phrase from your sermon. This will be a reminder of the message you wish them to carry on their hearts as they leave.

3. Allow the congregation to bless each other. For example, ask the congregation to turn to each other, look each other in the eye and repeat these words, "May the love of God / the grace of Christ / and the communion of the Holy Spirit / be with you all / now and forever, Amen" (2 Corinthians 13:14, adapted).

4. Use sacred gestures to enhance the meaning. You might consider the following postures and movements, or some variation of them.

❖ **Palm out:** Throughout the history of western religious art, Christ is often seen blessing others with his palm turned toward them. As you speak the benediction over the congregation, raise one or both hands with palms outward as a gesture of blessing.

❖ **Both arms out at forty-five degrees with wrist and hands toward your chest:** I experienced the effectiveness of this gesture at a concert given by a famous flamenco guitarist. As the audience applauded, he drew us in with this gesture as if to say, "We are all part of this experience."

❖ Direct the congregation in their own sacred action:

Direction: Looking up, arms and hands above the head, palms up. Bring both hands down to touch your forehead as the leader says ...

Blessing: May God bless you.

Direction: Cross arms over your chest with hands on shoulders.

Blessing: May Christ give you peace.

Direction: Cup both hands over your heart.

Blessing: And may the Holy Spirit give you comfort. And may the healing presence of Christ make you whole.

Direction: Extend both hands in front with palms up.

People's Response: Amen.

5. Ask the congregation to hold hands. As a symbol of the bond of love that unites worshipers throughout the week, ask the congregation to hold hands. The following are some suggestions for hand-clasped benedictions.

Say, "As a sign of your willingness to serve one another, extend your right hand to your side with the palm down. As a sign of your willingness to receive service and love from others, extend your left hand to your side with the palm up. In that way, hold hands with those next to you."

While holding hands, sing "Bind Us Together," "Bless Be the Tie That Binds," "We Are One in the Bond of Love," "The Servant Song," or another appropriate song that suggests our common bond as the body of Christ.

Suggestions for the Benediction Response

1. Lead the congregation in a song of parting. It is important to allow the congregation to respond to the benediction with an affirmation.

There are many appropriate dismissal songs for worship. Let the congregation sing their response with a "good word" of their own.

2. Recess during the benediction response. As the benediction response is being sung, all leaders on the platform including the choir recess down the center aisle. The first person down the aisle could carry a raised Christ candle as a sign of Christ going before us. This important symbol of the gathered church advancing back into the world will remind your congregation to follow Christ in service.

3. Recess behind dancers. Dance is a sign of joy and happiness. In the same way pilgrims of the Middle Ages danced their way out of the great cathedrals of Europe to begin their pilgrimage to Jerusalem, worshipers leave worship each week to journey into the surprising possibilities of daily life. Arrange for the morning recession to follow a dancer down the center aisle.

4. Leave worship in silence. Invite your worshipers to observe a silent recessional as they leave worship and maintain silence all the way to their cars. This is particularly effective during the Lenten season and Holy Week.

5. Offer prayer and anointing at the front of the sanctuary. As a response to the benediction, invite worshipers to come forward to meet with pastors and lay leaders for prayer. If someone is in need of healing, one minister should be prepared for the anointing of oil and the laying on of hands. This type of response requires a soft postlude or silence.

Postlude

THE WORD *POSTLUDE* COMES FROM THE Latin *postludium* and means "to play afterward." The postlude is not an afterthought or mere walking music. The postlude provides a transition from the security and power of God's holy presence to the challenges and opportunities of the week before us. As worshipers make a physical transition from the sanctuary to the foyer, the feeling created by the postlude music is what will stay with them as they leave.

Chapter 13

The Modulating Congregation

But once I become my own message
there is nothing else to hear.
No way to grow. No chance to change.
Nothing but echoes of my own voice.

Joan Chittister
Wisdom Distilled from the Daily, 25.

WHEN THE PSALMIST ADMONISHED GOD'S people to "sing a new song," the writer forgot to say that the new song may be in a different key. The psalmist also says nothing about the process of modulating from our present key to the new one. Any skilled musician will tell you it takes planning and skill to get from one key to another.

Modulation is an apt metaphor for how to deal with change in your church. If you want to be creative in worship, you necessarily have to initiate change. This will not be popular with all of the people all of the time. Yet innovation and change are necessary for growth. How to smooth the rough edges that change creates?

The dictionary defines *modulation* as "the process of moving from one key to another." The important word is process. Modulation doesn't just happen. If a musician jumps from one key to another without the process of modulation, the change is abrupt and jarring, leaving the listener stunned and frustrated.

Using that analogy of musical modulation, it's safe to say that most churches are modulating from one key to another in some area of church life. The process needs attention so that the church isn't stunned into a new key by abrupt change. Like skilled musicians, church leaders must plan and lead.

There are many ways to create a modulation. One popular method is to arrive at the dominant seventh chord of the new key. In the key of D, that would be A7. Here's an example. To modulate from the key of F to the key of D, use the following chord progression: F, Dm7, Em7, A7sus, A7, and finally D.

I give you this example to point out the most important part of resolving the modulation into the new key—dissonance. Without dissonance, there is no sense of resolution. Dissonance is a key ingredient in the process.

The suspension on the A7 chord creates a feeling of tension. When you move through the tension created by the suspended note to the A7 and then resolve the chord in a new key, there is an internal sigh of satisfaction and completion.

A musical friend told me that the wife of Richard Wagner, the great German composer, used to wake him in the morning by going to the piano and playing a phrase ending with an unresolved dominant seventh chord. He would then get out of bed, walk to the piano, and resolve the chord.

Tension, created by dissonance, is an important and necessary part of resolution. In the process of modulation, skilled church leaders anticipate and plan for tension in the congregation.

Change Can Hurt

Change happens. The physical world around us is changing all the time. Our bodies change each day. To sustain new life, organizations must accept change as a part of existence and make it their friend. A rut has been defined as "a grave with two open ends." Knowing when traditions are becoming ruts is an art that churches can and must learn.

For many people, change is experienced emotionally as loss. Loss creates grief. When grief is not validated and dealt with in a church, it leaks out in unhealthy and destructive ways. People who have been members of a church for many years and have built positive memories around certain patterns and traditions need love and care during times of transition and change so their grief does not hurt others. They are not prepared to "get out of bed and resolve the chord."

The Complex Composition of Churches
Traditional members are only one part of the equation. New staff members also have needs that come from grieving and letting go. Churches forget that new staff members may have served other congregations for years and bring their own attachments to worship traditions and programs. Those staff members have experienced loss and need to be heard lest their enthusiasm quickly dies.

New members have little attachment to current programs and traditions. They bring fresh ideas and energy to the church but too often are stifled by the firmly entrenched traditions that long-time members enjoy.

Young people have their own set of evolving needs and desires. What is exciting and inviting to them in worship might be frightening to someone else with a more traditional point of view. Young families, single parents, those in mid-life transition and retirees all have differing, sometimes conflicting needs, attachments, and desires. The body of Christ is a complex organism. Fortunately, our love for Christ is what unites us rather than shared taste in music and worship style.

It has been said, "Change is inevitable, but growth is a choice." Here are some proven principles to help your church choose life and grow stronger and richer through modulation and change.

Suggestions for Growth through Modulation

1. Resist the temptation to create separate congregations defined by style. Offering a variety of worship services defined by style is a popular and often successful church growth tool. The premise makes sense. It goes like this, "When it comes to style in worship, opposites do not attract. People are attracted to those who like what they like. By offering a smorgasbord of worship services according to style, comfort zones are created. Those who like Bach go to the traditional service, those who like rock go to the contemporary service." No question, this method may help your church add numbers because people prefer choices.

But is the motto of the church, "the customer is always right"? Worshipers are not clients. Churches are in the business of creating a new heaven and a new earth, not satisfying share holders. The church is the body of Christ, knit together in love. Growth and maturity come from the process of listening to each other's point of view, understanding each other's emotions and working through conflict. Segregating people according to their musical and stylistic tastes may grow numbers but it will not grow depth. Depth and maturity is the key to a new heaven and a new earth.

2. Move beyond tolerance. Tolerance is a beginning, but it is incomplete. Jesus did not say, "the world will know you are my disciples if you tolerate each other." As Jesus' disciples, love is the virtue we seek. Tolerance usually means that we bear or put up with someone or something we don't like. Love, on the other hand, is a decision to understand, respect and desire the best for another person. As we worship together, love allows us to celebrate a style we dislike knowing it creates an open heart for someone else.

3. Celebrate diversity. Diversity can be defined as the unique and dissimilar characteristics that create variety. The word community means "with unity." Unless there is diversity, there is nothing to unite. Hence, without diversity there is no community.

We discover true community in the process of understanding differences and of choosing unity that is based on those differences. This shared process of understanding how we each open our hearts to God in worship in a unique way characterizes the "modulating church."

4. Make a church-wide commitment to variety in worship. Variety is the spice of life. This adage is true unless I don't like your spices. Some church members have developed an allergy to certain spices. There are those who are allergic to a classic prelude and others who break out in hives around a drum set. How can we find unity in the midst of this diversity? We set the stage by placing our musical ducks in a row.

❖ Make sure your musicians can play a particular style of music with integrity. It is the rare musician who can play all styles of music authentically. A praise song written with contemporary instruments in mind should not be played with organ accompaniment. This would be like asking a rock band to play a Handel organ concerto. It's music, but it lacks stylistic integrity. Organists bring their own unique skills as do other kinds of keyboard artists and all other musicians. You may need more than one keyboard player to use all the different styles of music you want to use.

❖ If your church has a traditional worship style and is modulating into variety, think carefully before you allow an acoustic drum set in your sanctuary. If you have a drummer and you want to add drums to your contemporary music, buy an electronic drum set. This will allow your drummer to play, but will give your sound technician control over the sound mix. In an age of techno-sound, electronic drums provide the necessary sounds without the jarring change an acoustic set creates. Traditional church members are deathly allergic to acoustic drum sets. There is no known antidote.

❖ Integrate new styles slowly and carefully. Many churches say they "blend" diverging styles of worship into one service. I applaud a confluence of style, but this is not blending, which the dictionary defines as "to mix or fuse thoroughly, so that the parts merge and are no longer distinct." It is not the goal of the modulating church to make style indistinct. Our goal is to build community by celebrating variety in all its fullness. This is accomplished by understanding what makes each style unique. For example, when you teach the congregation a new song, teach something about its composer, the culture represented by the musical style, and what makes it worth learning. If you can't articulate these ingredients, you're not ready to teach the song.

5. Create ways for different "cultures" of members to understand each other. Criminologists will tell you that anonymity encourages violence; road rage is an obvious current example. If a person cuts in front of you in your local grocery store, chances are slim that you'll fly into a rage in those familiar surroundings. But if that happens in the anonymous setting of a crowded highway, it's too often a different story. This may seem an extreme example for this idea, but the point is the same. The closer people are to you, the more you see them as your friends. The farther away they are, the easier it is to mistake them for enemies.

Provide creative ways for members to cross the lines of generations. For example, you might invite your members to a church "block party." After dinner, show the video "The Greatest Generation" by Tom Brokaw and provide ways for young people to enter the hearts of your "seasoned citizens." Friendly informative get-togethers like this will have a positive impact on the process of integrating various styles in worship.

Chapter 14

Cleaning Up:
Frequently Asked Questions

What about children in worship?
Where should the announcements be placed?
Is applause appropriate in worship?

What about Children in Worship

In this context, children means kindergarten through fifth grade. Pastoral leaders and worship committees need to decide whether or not to include these children in worship. If a church decides to include children, church leaders need to have a strategy for integrating them and valuing their gifts. If a church would rather educate children outside the adult worship environment, they should affirm that decision and create programs of quality for children in their own setting.

Either way, a comprehensive approach to worship education and participation is needed for children in the church. Churches lacking a strategic approach will not serve their children well.

In many churches, worship leaders offer a specific experience for children, often called the "children's sermon." In this style, children are usually invited to come to the front of the sanctuary for a sermon or an object lesson designed for them. Following the

> *Children in Worship*
> *Obedience to Christ demands a peculiar concern for children among us. It would be ironic indeed if we consider the welfare of children in every area except that most central point in our life—worship.*
>
> David Ng and Virginia Thomas
> Children in the Worshiping Community, 3

story, they either go back to their seats or are sent out of the sanctuary for "children's church."

Adults leaving worship are often heard to say, "I got more out of the children's sermon today than the regular sermon." That statement defines the problem with this approach.

Child development experts tell us that children under the age of twelve think in concrete terms, much like the writers of the Old Testament. For example, the Hebrew writers described God as a rock or a fortress, or even as a bush. Those visual images are easy for children to understand. However, we must remember that, for children, God remains a rock or a fortress. They don't have a need to interpret the meaning of those images and make an application in their life.

Adults, on the other hand, think more abstractly, much like the writers of the New Testament. For those Greek writers, God becomes spirit. Adults easily interpret that concept in a variety of abstract ways and apply that meaning to their lives, especially with the help of an object lesson in the children's story.

If we want to value children and their learning style, the children's sermon should be a story told directly to the children, not through the children to the adults. Too often, children are used as a way to educate and entertain adult on-lookers. Consider the following suggestions for cultivating more effective inclusion of children in your worship services.

1. Plan carefully. If you choose to include a specific time for children to come forward in worship, place it appropriately in the framework of the liturgy—the service of the word. Make it part of the Scripture and sermon. This placement of the "children's story" indicates that God desires to speak directly to children as well as adults in worship.

2. Include children in the planning and leading of worship. If we believe children are a vital part of the body of Christ today, ask them for input into worship. Find out what they like most about worship. Discover what they like to do in worship. Ask about their favorite music.

Many children are capable of reading in public, including printed prayers, litanies, and Scripture. Rehearse with them ahead of time so they have a successful experience.

3. Include illustrations, songs, and readings that make sense to children. If children remain in worship for the sermon, include illustrations and songs from children's television, movies, and literature. If children make personal connections throughout the service, they will feel welcome and more involved in the worship experience.

Where Should the Announcements Be Placed?

If we take a broad view of our identity as the people of God, we must affirm that we are not only the church at worship on Sunday mornings, but we are also the church in service during the week. Announcements support the life of the congregation and make it possible for people to be involved in service throughout the week ahead; they are indeed a necessary part of worship.

If you structure worship around the fourfold pattern of the liturgy, the most appropriate place for announcements is just before worshipers leave the sanctuary to return to the world. Welcoming visitors and registering attendance, which are often part of the announcements, could be placed creatively at the beginning of the service during the gathering instead. In rethinking the placement of your announcements, keep these suggestions in mind.

1. Don't waste good drama on announcements. Teach the congregation that drama has a special place in worship and will be used to enhance their understanding and insight. Chances are good that attendance for the church dinner or work day will not increase in proportion to the excellence of any dramatic effect used to announce it. Someone may, however, hear scripture through drama in a way that will have a life-changing impact.

2. Make a list of announcements available in printed form. To minimize the need for spoken announcements in worship, create an attractive printed brochure each week with churchwide opportunities listed. Hand this it out with the weekly bulletin.

3. Use e-mail. Reminders can easily be sent to the congregation over the Internet. Create e-mail address lists of your members and send announcements during the week.

Is Applause Appropriate in Worship?

Pastors and worship committees need to think this issue through carefully. This question is more complex than we would like to admit. In the process of socialization, most people in the Western world have been taught to clap their open palms together if they like what they have just heard or seen. In many cultures, this is an accepted way of showing appreciation.

When people are inspired in worship or want to show appreciation for the youth choir's hard work with a difficult song, they instinctively use the means they have been taught to show their affirmation. They applaud. That exchange of energy between worship leaders and the congregation is a good thing. We're glad the congregation is listening and responding.

However, we live in a culture of entertainment. We applaud often and in many situations. Does such a performance-oriented response belong in a worship service? If we do *not* want applause in worship, we need to offer creative alternatives for congregational response in emotional situations and teach those alternatives to our congregations. We cannot expect them to be satisfied with a simple, "Don't do that." Remember these suggestions when considering this issue for your congregation.

1. Hold an open church forum to discuss the applause response in worship. You may want to invite ministry colleagues from different cultural settings. This will give your congregation other perspectives on the subject. You may also want to bring in a consultant to lead the discussion with the congregation. The facilitator should be able to provide an outside, objective voice, thereby removing the pastoral staff from the "hot seat." During the forum, these questions will guide you:

❖ What does applause mean to you in the context you personally represent? (e.g., ethnicity, family background, neighborhood, culture, denomination, region of the country)

❖ What are the differences between hand clapping in worship (e.g., during singing and praising) and applause for a presentation or a performance?

❖ How do you define performance? Is there a place for performance in worship? (For a balanced discussion of performance in worship, I recommend *The New Worship: Straight Talk on Music and the Church* by Barry Leisch.)

❖ Is applause ever appropriate at any point in the service?

❖ Can you identify places in the order of service where applause or hand clapping is more appropriate or less appropriate?

❖ If not applause, what are appropriate emotional congregational responses in worship?

❖ If your congregation affirms applause in worship, are there any boundaries or guidelines?

❖ If your congregation frowns on applause in worship, in what other ways can worshipers respond in a spontaneous way?

2. Make a decision and articulate it to the congregation. For some congregations, the applause response is a normal part of the flow between the worshiper and those on the platform. For others, it is not. Make a conscious decision about this custom with your specific church in mind. You can do this in an open church forum, as suggested above, or among the church leadership. Whether you decide "for" or "against" applause in your worship services, that decision must be clearly and graciously communicated to the congregation. This is particularly important if you decide "against." In an entertainment-oriented culture, it is inappropriate to assume people will instinctively hold their applause in worship. If you do not want the congregation to applaud, note that clearly in the printed order of worship. If there is no printed bulletin, give a gracious verbal instruction to the congregation at the beginning of each worship service.

3. Offer alternatives to applause. Applause indicates a desire to respond to an inspirational presentation. If you decide against applause, give your congregation other effective ways to respond.

❖ Place a printed post card in the pew rack and indicate it is for positive response or feedback for any element of the worship service. As worshipers feel led to respond, they can write a note to a leader or other participant telling them that they appreciate their ministry. This card could be placed in the offering plate or given to an usher at the end of the service. The church office can address these cards and mail them.

❖ When something significant has just happened in worship, and it is obvious that people need to respond to the work of the Spirit in their midst, ask the congregation to say "Amen" together. This will provide the necessary release of energy and affirmation.

More active and spontaneous responses might include:

❖ Stand up as a sign of your affirmation.

❖ "Talk back" with words of encouragement and agreement.

❖ Raise both hands high and waving above your head.

❖ As a sign of individual receptivity, place both hands on your lap with palms up.

❖ Kneel as a sign of your awareness of God's presence through the presentation or performance.

Appendix A

The Gift of Liturgical Time

WALKING IN AND OUT OF STORES AND SHOPPING malls throughout the year, I'm struck by the way our culture tells time. It's impossible to miss. The cultural clock ticks through the marketing seasons with ceremonial precision. The chronology is enhanced by colors. Put red roses, red boxes of chocolate, and red streamers in the aisle, and shoppers know Valentine's Day is almost here. By contrast, March is the green month for St. Patrick's Day. While Christians in Ireland crowd into church for Mass, North Americans endure life-sized leprechauns, corned beef, and green beer. And on it goes.

This cultural calendar is what I call the Hallmark Year. Based on commerce and greeting cards, it has its own "holy days": New Year's Day, Martin Luther King Jr. Day, Presidents' Day, St. Patrick's Day, Secretaries' Day, Mother's Day, Memorial Day, Flag Day, Father's Day, Children's Day, Independence Day, Labor Day, Bosses' Day, Halloween, Veteran's Day, Thanksgiving, Christmas Day, and New Year's Eve. The pressure to celebrate these days is obvious; many of them are based on important relationships and cultural memories.

Christian organizations add to the pressure. Denominations are organizations with needs and agendas. Therefore, denominational planning calendars both reflect their own cultural time and add more special days: Boy Scout Sunday, Bible Sunday, Youth Sunday, Chaplain's Sunday, Seminary Sunday, Mission Sunday, Peace Sunday,

Women's Sunday, Men's Sunday, and Laity Sunday.

The motivation behind this pressure should be scrutinized. The icons of national pride or religious culture must not inform the way the body of Christ orders its worship and keeps its calendar. The greatest single step toward the revitalization of worship is congregational planning and organizing according to the Christian year and the lectionary.

The lectionary is a systematized way of organizing Scripture for its use in worship. For each Sunday, three lessons are assigned: one from the Hebrew Scriptures, one from the Epistles and one from the Gospels. When all three lessons are read, the three-year cycle of the lectionary is designed to complete most of the Christian Scriptures and large portions of the Hebrew Scriptures.

Following the Roman Catholic Church's Second Vatican Council, which concluded in 1964, a group of scholars and consultants from many denominations developed the Revised Common Lectionary, what James F. White, in his *Introduction to Christian Worship*, calls, "the most carefully prepared lectionary in all Christian history" (White, 70). This ecumenical lectionary has since been adapted for use in many denominations, but its content and style remain true to its ecumenical intent.

Seasons of the Church Year

The church's unique way of telling time is the Christian year. There are six seasons, each placing the worshiper in a different chapter of Jesus' life.

1. Advent. The first season of the church year, Advent begins on the Sunday nearest November 30 and includes the four Sundays before Christmas. The word advent means "coming." During the season of Advent, Christians prepare themselves for the coming of Christ. The Advent color is purple, suggesting the royal nature of Christ.

2. Christmastide. Christmas, the second season of the church year, begins on December 25, Christmas Day, and lasts twelve days. White and gold express the joyous nature of this season.

3. Epiphany. Epiphany begins on January 6 and continues until Ash Wednesday. The Greek *epiphaneia* means "appearing into." During Epiphany, Christians remember the story of the three magi who gave gifts to the infant Jesus and then took the good news of his birth across the world. It also commemorates the beginning of Jesus' ministry. Green, the color of this season, expresses the timeless nature of growth.

4. Lent. Lent begins on Ash Wednesday and continues for forty days (not including Sundays) until Easter. During Lent, Christians remember how Jesus fasted for forty days in the wilderness and how the ancient Hebrews wandered for forty years in the desert. The word Lent comes from the Middle English for "spring." So in the midst of the wilderness, we anticipate the joy of resurrection and new life. The traditional color of this season is purple.

5. Eastertide. Easter is the season in which Christians celebrate Jesus' resurrection from the dead. This season begins on Easter Sunday, which is the first Sunday after the first full moon after the vernal equinox (March 21). White is the traditional color for Eastertide, which lasts for fifty days.

6. Pentecost or Ordinary Time. Pentecost is the day on which the disciples received the Holy Spirit. Coming from the Greek word that means "fiftieth day," Pentecost is celebrated on the fiftieth day after Easter. Red, symbolizing tongues of fire, is the color of the day.

Also known as Kingdomtide or the season of Pentecost, ordinary time is celebrated from Pentecost Sunday to the first Sunday of Advent. Green is the color for this season.

The Gifts of Liturgical Time

1. Affirmation of Jesus as Lord. As Christians, one of our basic affirmations is "Jesus is Lord." Ordering worship according to the events of Jesus' life provides a specific way for a congregation to make Jesus Lord. Planning according to "the Hallmark year" keeps us focused away from Christ.

Study the way your congregation plans and organizes. Use these questions to consider your commitment to the Christian year.

❖ Does the church year begin with January 1 or does it begin with Advent? Do you celebrate the Christmas season or, like our culture, is Christmas one day long?

❖ Within the seasons of the church year there are many special Sundays. Do you ever hear or preach a sermon on the baptism of Christ? The baptism of our Lord is usually celebrated in January on the Sunday following Epiphany Sunday. This would be an appropriate day on which to schedule baptisms and to celebrate a congregational reaffirmation of baptismal vows. The liturgical color is white.

❖ Does your church know anything about Transfiguration Sunday? It is marked during the season of Epiphany and the liturgical color is white. This special Sunday celebrates the transfiguration of Jesus, described in Matthew 17 and Mark 9. In a sense, that Gospel story is about the disciples finally seeing Jesus as he really was—the Incarnation of God. How could celebrating the transfiguration of Christ once a year benefit your congregation? Or perhaps your celebration might focus on the transfiguration of the disciples' sight. How is our sight clouded today by our own preconceptions and limited experiences?

❖ Ascension Sunday is celebrated the Sunday before Pentecost. This Sunday marks the day when Jesus left his disciples, entrusting them with the continuation of his earthly work (Acts 1:6-11). It is appropriately celebrated just before Pentecost because just before he ascended, Jesus promised his followers the gift of the Holy Spirit, the power to carry on his mission and ministry. What does the ascension of Christ mean in a person's life?

❖ How does Pentecost Sunday, which commemorates the baptism of the Holy Spirit in Acts 2, affect church life? What is the role of the Holy Spirit in the life of your church?

2. Understanding Jesus' life as a metaphor. When my young son was diagnosed with a brain tumor, Jesus' life as a metaphor became an important understanding for me. I no longer thought of

Jesus as an untouchable God to be admired and worshiped. I saw Jesus as the most authentic human being, teaching us what life is about. I realized that my life runs parallel to Jesus' life. Many of his choices will become my choices, his experiences my experiences. Through my observance of the Christian year, I began to see that Holy Week was an affirmation of Christ's solidarity with my family's pain. Lent was our wilderness; Good Friday, our death; resurrection, our hope. Jesus walked there before us to walk with us now. The Christian year offers a metaphor for life.

3. The expansion of preaching. The lectionary forces preachers to expand their repertoire. Its comprehensive approach to Scripture calls us beyond our pet topics and favorite passages. The lectionary brings with it an accountability to the totality of Scripture that will keep worship planners and preachers challenged and stimulated.

4. Built-in ecumenism. Preaching from the ecumenical lectionary keeps us connected to Christians down the street and around the world. Lutherans, Baptists, Episcopalians, Methodists, Roman Catholics, and others who use the same lectionary all focus their worship on the same Sunday Scripture readings. Even with slight variations, this united approach provides one more step toward reconciliation and cooperation.

5. Facilitation of planning. In the practical world, using the lectionary provides the possibility for planning a year or more, making coordination among the many ministries in the church possible. Cooperative efforts among preachers, musicians and worship planners will go a long way toward creating good will among staff members. Because of the widespread use of the lectionary, many fine resources have been created to assist worship leaders in their planning. If you've never used these resources before, you'll find they can enrich your congregation's worship beyond anything you can imagine.

Appendix B
A Home Dedication Service

*Between the foundation and the roof of the
Christian home, ... church community comes
alive. No two domestic churches are identical,
but they all share in the intimacy of incarnate
divinity and so present to the entire Church
and to the world the human face and
vital activity of God's own life.*

—*Wendy Wright,*
Sacred Dwelling, 26

ONE OF THE DEFINITIONS OF *HOME* IS, "THE
place where one likes to be." That description rings true for me. As
a pastor, one of the joys of my job is meeting with people in their
homes. The apartment or house they purchased or built was a simple dwelling place until they made it their own. It wasn't their home
until they took the time to re-create the space by surrounding themselves with the things that defined them and gave their life meaning
like family pictures, gifts, unique paintings, furniture they enjoy, family heirlooms and mementos. For many people, home is an extension
of their soul and becomes the container for their life experience.

For this reason, dedicating this important living space to God's loving protection and care is a helpful ritual. Each room in the home has significant symbolic meaning attached to the routines and experiences of our daily lives. As you walk through the house, emphasize that meaning and apply it to the spiritual journey of those who dwell there.

The following is an example of adapting a service to fit your needs. This particular service was adapted from Edward Hays' book, *Prayers for the Domestic Church: A Handbook for Worship in the Home.*

<hr />

Home Dedication Service

All gather in the living room.

Opening Remarks

Make brief opening remarks about our homes as a sacred dwelling. For example:

Welcome to this open home. We have gathered here today to celebrate this place and to dedicate it and its new occupants to God's loving care. All that God has created is good and holy. We are here, as family and friends, to call forth a special grace from God to use this home as its artistic Creator intended. And we are here to bless those who will live within its walls; to bless them as receivers of light, love, and special affirmation from God; and to awaken them to experience how God uses the ordinary events of life to touch us with divine love.

May this service of dedication strengthen the inhabitants of this home and deepen their love for one another in this place.

Opening Prayer

(Read aloud by the inhabitants of the house.)

Dear God:

May this house be a sacred dwelling for those who live here.

May those who visit here feel the peace we have received from you.

May darkness not enter.

May the light of God shield this house from harm.

May the angels bring their peace here and use our home as a haven of light.

May all grow strong in this place of healing, our sanctuary from the noise of the world.

May it be used by you forever.

Amen.

All move to the breezeway/entryway, saying together:

Bless this entryway. May all who come here be treated with respect and kindness. May all our comings and goings be under God's loving care.

Sing together a song of invocation or blessing, such as "Come and Fill Our Hearts with Your Peace" (in Songs and Prayers from Taizé), *changing the words, "our hearts" to "this home."*

All move to the living room, saying together:

Blessed be this living room. May we live within it as people of peace. May contemplative prayer and playfulness never be strangers within these walls. May the spirits of love and affection together with the spirits of angelic care touch all who shall live in this room.

Sing together a song of invocation or blessing.

All move to dining room, saying together:

Blessed be this gathering place for food and family life. May all our meals be sacraments in the presence of God as we are nourished at this table.

Sing together a song of invocation or blessing.

All move to kitchen, saying together:

Blessed be this shrine of the kitchen. Blessed be the herbs and spices, the pots, pans, and dishes that shall prepare our meals. May the ill-seasonings of anger and bitterness never poison the meals prepared here.

Sing together a song of invocation or blessing.

All move to master bedroom, saying together:

Blessed be this master bedroom suite. Here may one find rest, refreshment, and renewal.

Sing together a song of invocation or blessing.

All move to family room and study, saying together:

Blessed be this family room and study. May it offer a place of togetherness, fun, and intellectual inquiry.

Sing together a song of invocation or blessing.

Move in turn to each of the remaining bedrooms, naming each occupant and saying together:

Blessed be _____'s room. May he/she find rest, refreshment and renewal here.

Sing together a song of invocation or blessing.

Move to the music room, saying together:

Blessed be this music room. May the music created here echo in sound and vibration to become a healing balm to performer and listener alike.

Sing together a song of invocation or blessing.

All move to the youth game/entertainment space, saying together:

Blessed be this teenage hangout. May the joy of living be abundant here, may our young people feel welcomed and safe here, and may there be harmony and rest within.

Sing together a song of invocation or blessing.

All move to the bathroom(s), saying together:

Blessed be this bathroom (or powder room).
May a spirit of health and healing abide here
and teach us to honor and care for our bodies.
May the cleansing of impurities remind us of our need
to let go of negative thoughts and critical attitudes
toward ourselves and others.

Sing together a song of invocation or blessing.

All return to the living room.
Provide an opportunity for those gathered to give a personal bless-
ing over the inhabitants.
Silent Prayer

Pastoral Prayer

(To be prayed by a person of inhabitant's choosing)

Lord our God—may your divine name be always holy within this home. May you as Creator lovingly care for all who shall live here. May your kingdom come in this home. May the people who live here live in harmony and unity. May they never suffer from lack of bread or from lack of what is needed to nourish the family. May the spirit of pardon and forgiveness reside here and be always ready to heal divisions. May the spirit of mirth and laughter, hope and faith, playfulness and prayer, compassion and love be perpetual guests in this home.

Inhabitants' Response

May our door always be open to those in need—to the neighbor and the stranger. May our friends who come to us in times of trouble or sorrow find the door open to them and their needs. May the holy light of God's presence shine forth brightly in this home and be a blessing to all those who shall live or rest here, and for everyone who comes to this door. May the doors of our hearts be open to God's indwelling presence. May God's holy blessing rest upon us all.

All sing again a song of invocation or blessing. *If you have elected to use "Come and Fill Our Hearts with Your Peace," sing it three times. The first time, change the words, "our hearts" to "this home." The second time, change the words to "these friends." The third and final time, change the lyric to "this world."*

Appendix C
A Healing Prayer Service

Healer of our every ill,
light of each tomorrow,
Give us peace beyond our fear,
and hope beyond our sorrow.

Marty Haugen, *"Healer of Our Every Ill"*

ONE OF THE MOST UNDERSTATED ASPECTS OF THE word *salvation* is the root word "salve." This etymology leads us to the related concepts of medicine and healing. When salvation is considered in this way, we view the saving work of Jesus as a journey into wholeness. We see, then, the process of salvation as a gradual healing of body, mind, and spirit. Instead of the dramatic, immediate conversion experience associated with a "cure," the nondramatic journey toward healing is filled with progressive, inner transformations that lead, in time, to long term health and fulfillment.

With this understanding of healing in mind, those who care about the salvation of others take on the symbolic role of "nurse practitioners." In his book *Care of the Soul,* Thomas Moore suggests that "care is what a nurse does, and 'nurse' happens to be one

> *Health is a state of complete physical, mental and social well-being and not merely the absence of disease or infirmity.*
>
> Constitution of the World Health Organization

of the early meanings of the Greek word therapeia, or therapy" (5).

If one aspect of salvation is the process of healing, then worship and prayer that are focused on inner restoration and wholeness become an important ongoing ministry of the church. Many Gospel stories describe Jesus' own emphasis on healing. Clearly, leading people to wholeness in body, mind, and spirit was a significant part of Christ's earthly mission. Through services of healing prayer, the church continues that ministry.

Preparation for a Service of Healing Prayer

1. Cleansing. Prepare a bowl of warm water with rose oil and rose petals. Place this bowl and a towel on a stand near the entrance to the chapel or sanctuary. Put the following sign near the bowl:

As a symbol of your own vulnerability
and God's cleansing power,
we invite you to wash your hands as you enter.

2. Candlelight. Make the chapel's atmosphere warm and inviting. Use candles as more than decoration; the flame is a point of identification for us as the light of Christ. Edward Hays suggests, "even the small and simple flame of a single candle can be a very important ally in your prayer. . . . A flickering flame can help make your prayer dance" *(Prayers for a Planetary Pilgrim,* 238).

3. Simplicity. Those who are coming to pray will inevitably bring with them the complexity of trauma, illness, and pain. Simplicity is the key to a healing prayer space. In addition to candles, a simple cross or bouquet of flowers is enough.

4. Meaning. As part of the service, provide meaningful ritual and singing. Participants need to be invited to take part in the service. Use words to guide, instruct and pray, not to preach.

5. Familiarity. Tradition is comforting to those who are grieving. In this setting, introduce new songs with care. Well-known songs of comfort will be well received and most appropriate.

Order of Worship for a Service of Healing Prayer

Call to Worship: Evening Prayer, solo, Marty Haugen
Prayer of Beginning
Song: O Lord, Hear My Prayer, Taizé Congregation
Scripture Reading: Matthew 11:28-30
Song: (familiar, comforting song here)
Guided Meditation or Prayer (see possibilities below)
Response (see possibilities below)
Scripture Reading (in unison): Psalm 23
Benediction

Possibilities for Guided Meditation

1. Touch. As participants enter, give each one a rock at least the size of a lemon. Lead a meditation on the theme of "God is my rock." Have them touch the rock and really look at it as you guide them through the meditation. Make comparisons between the rock, their life, and God's presence. End with a unison reading of Psalm 62:6-8.

2. See. Hand out a photograph or project a slide of the Isenheim Altarpiece painted in 1515 by Matthias Grünewald. Painted during the plague for a hospital chapel in France, Christ is depicted on the cross, covered with sores such as the ones afflicting those suffering from the plague. Lead a meditation on Christ's identification with our pain. Give them silent time to "be with" the altarpiece.

3. Write. As participants enter, hand out paper and pencil. Invite them to write their own psalm of lament using these six components:

- *Address* it to the Lord (cry out to God)
- Include a *plea* for help (identify your need)
- Offer a *complaint* (give God the specifics of your situation)
- Say something about your *confidence* in God's presence, love, and grace (express your trust)
- Offer *thanksgiving* to God (*in* all things, not necessarily *for* all things)
- Conclude with a *doxology* to God (hymn of praise)

Possibilities for Congregational Response

1. The laying on of hands. Invite participants to come forward one at a time for prayer. People can stand, kneel, or sit as they receive prayer. (Make sure a chair is nearby for those who wish or need to sit.) As the leader moves into place near the one who has come, invite anyone else present who would like to pray to come forward, gently placing hands on the one requesting prayer. Offer this prayer, asking those around you to repeat each phrase after you pray. A healing prayer could be as simple as this: "Loving God (pause for others to repeat), Creator of _____ (pause), bring about her/his healing (pause) as you would have it (pause). In the name of Jesus we pray (pause). Amen."

2. Singing with movement. Songs with motions are too often allowed only with children. But even simple movements can help embody the message of a song. "Healer of My Soul" written by John Michael Talbot is a beautiful song of healing. I use the modified version of the song provided below. Hand motions add power to its beauty. Play the CD or sing it together, supplying printed lyrics to each participant. Sing it through with them once, demonstrating hand motions such as those described below.

Healer of my soul.
Heal me *at even. Heal* me *at morning. Heal* me *at noon.*
Healer of my soul.

The first time through the song, sing "Healer of *my soul* ... Heal *me*," with cupped hands over your own heart. The second time, sing "Healer of *our souls* … Heal *us*," and as a sign of unity and solidarity, take the hand of the person next to you on each side while you sing. Finally, sing "Healer of *their souls* … Heal *them*," and hold your hands out in front of you with palms up—offering others to God across time and space.

Appendix *D*

Worship and Prayer in the Style of the Taizé Community

One passes through Taizé
as one passes close to a spring of water.

—Pope John Paul II

MY PILGRIMAGE TO THE TAIZÉ COMMUNITY began in an unusual place. Westminster Choir College in Princeton, New Jersey is known for its excellent choral program, brilliant faculty and the presence of world-class organists. Since I was studying music, I did not expect to experience a prayer form that would captivate my heart for the next eighteen years. Then one morning, our class was introduced to the music and prayer of Taizé.

The prayer began with singing a simple eight-bar phrase and these words, "Jesus, remember me when you come into your kingdom." As I sang, I focused first on the words, identifying with the one who spoke them to Jesus—the thief on the cross. However, with each repetition I found myself relaxing deeper into the presence of Christ, the one to whom I sang.

Occasionally, an oboe or cello would add an obligato to the singing. Singers began adding choral parts until all four parts wrapped around my soul as a cloak. As I sang in that community of musicians, I prayed in a way I'd never prayed before. Fourteen years later, I finally walked into the crowded sanctuary of the Church of the Reconciliation on a hilltop in Burgundy, France, and sang that prayer with people from other nations around the world.

The Community

Taizé is a village in the Burgundy region of France. Roger Schütz, son of a Swiss Protestant minister, was only twenty-five years old when he came to Taizé from Switzerland in 1940. In the war-torn years that followed, he began sheltering Jewish refugees and praying in the village church. Others joined him and soon a small community of brothers was formed.

Believing there would always be war in Europe until Christians stopped killing Christians, Roger and his followers committed themselves to a ministry of reconciliation, a challenging and difficult task in postwar France and Germany. Slowly, one by one, brothers

Taizé-style Prayer

Nothing is more conducive to a communion with the living God than a meditative common prayer with, as its high point, singing that never ends and that continues in the silence of one's heart when one is alone again. When the mystery of God becomes tangible through the simple beauty of symbols, when it is not smothered by too many words, then a common prayer, far from exuding monotony and boredom, awakens us to heaven's joy on earth.

Brother Roger of Taizé
Songs & Prayers from Taizé, 7

> *From the depths of the human condition a secret aspiration rises up. Caught up in the anonymous rhythms of schedules and timetables, men and women of today are implicitly thirsting for the one essential reality: an inner life, signs of the invisible.*
>
> Brother Roger of Taizé

began making lifelong commitments to communal life. Donning white robes, adopting a Benedictine style of daily life, and receiving Roman Catholic, Orthodox, and Protestant brothers from many countries, Taizé has become a monastic model of ecumenism. Roger refers to this community as a "pilgrimage of trust on earth."

Over the years that followed, young people from all over Europe made their way to Taizé to open themselves to this communion that gives meaning to their lives. Today, from May to October, as many as six thousand young people a week come to Taizé for the weekly meetings with the brothers. Focusing on three periods of communal prayer each day, participants delve into the meaning of their own spiritual journey, explore their faith commitments, and worship with people from all over the world.

The Music and Prayer

Contemplation has been described as a "long loving gaze at what is real." Worship at Taizé is contemplative in its style in that it gives the worshiper time to focus on God's presence within and without. Much of the praying is in silence. Taizé music is composed in an ostinato pattern—a short, simple phrase repeated many times. Often a Scripture text and sometimes a quotation attributed to a devout person, each phrase expresses an essential reality, quickly understood by the intellect, which is then integrated slowly into one's attitude and actions.

Instrumentalists pray through their playing by adding an obligato above the communal singing. Descants—often a psalm—are also sung above the chant. One song may take as long as five minutes. In this atmosphere of simplicity and focused attention, one is free to "rest" in the presence of God.

For years, many of the songs written for the Taizé community were written by one of the brothers, Jacques Berthier. Following his death, French Jesuit priest Joseph Gelineau has composed new chants for the community.

CDs, cassettes, and printed music from Taizé are available for purchase online at www.illuminatedjourneys.com or by calling 877-489-8500. Worship workshops in the style of Taizé are available for your church or organization. Call Illuminated Journeys for more information.

Guidelines for Creating Worship in the Taizé Style

1. Create a peaceful, inviting focal point for worship. Use a cross, candles, plants and icons.

2. Place musicians off to the side in a circle. There is no visible leadership in this style of worship. If the service is held in a large room, the musicians should be miked so all vocal parts can be heard. This provides support for the participants. Musicians should rehearse before the service.

3. Participants should be invited to enter in silence. This gives everyone permission not to talk to each other. Use signs at the entrances of the church to accomplish this goal.

Prayer takes us by surprise: even if all kinds of contradictions and doubts are still there, a longing comes to light, and the silence reveals a peace close at hand ... It sets the heart free and releases a surge of new life.

Taizé: Trust on Earth, 1

4. To support participants in their silence, write suggestions for silent prayer on a sheet of paper to be picked up as people come in.
5. Prayers and Scriptures are read from the side of the room or from the back. Keep the focus away from the person reading so it will stay on the text that is read.
6. In Taizé worship, the sermon is replaced by silent meditation.

Order of Worship for Taizé-Style Worship Service

Song: "Veni Sancte Spiritus", # 41–*Songs and Prayers from Taizé*
Song: "Sing, Praise and Bless the Lord" #35–*Songs and Prayers from Taizé*
Scripture: Psalm 139:1-6,13-18
(As the psalm is read, light the Christ candle as a symbol of Christ's presence)
Song: "Lord Jesus Christ", #15–*Taizé: Songs for Prayer*
Silence: (10 minutes)
Scripture: Matthew 18:21-35
Song: "God Can Only Give Faithful Love", #57–*Taizé: Songs for Prayer*
Scripture: Romans 14:1-12
Silence: (10 Minutes)
Song: "Nada te Turbe", #29–*Songs and Prayers from Taizé*
Prayer of Petition and Thanksgiving
"Kyrie (Lord have mercy)", #4–*Songs and Prayers from Taizé*
Song: "Jesus, Remember Me", #11–*Taizé: Songs for Prayer*
Silence (10 minutes)
The Lord's Prayer
Song: "In God Alone", #19–*Songs and Prayers from Taizé*
Song: "In the Lord", #47–*Songs and Prayers from Taizé*

During the last song, someone carries the lighted Christ candle down the aisle and out the back door as a sign of Christ leading us back into the world to love and serve.

Bibliography

Elizabeth Achtemeier. *Creative Preaching: Finding the Words.* Abingdon Preaching Library. William D. Thompson, ed. Nashville: Abingdon Press, 1980.

Mary Ellen Ashcroft. *Dogspell: A Dogmatic Theology on the Abounding Love of God.* Leavenworth, Kans.: Forest of Peace Publishing, 2000.

Joseph Cardinal Bernardin. "Foreword," in *The Collegeville Hymnal.* Edward J. McKenna, ed. Collegeville, Minn.: The Liturgical Press, 1990.

Andrew W. Blackwood. *The Fine Art of Public Worship.* Nashville: Abingdon Press, 1939.

Jean M. Blomquist. "Daily Dancing with the Holy One," in *Weavings.* Vol. IV, no. 6.

Frederick Buechner. *Wishful Thinking: A Theological ABC.* New York: Harper & Row Publishers, 1973.

Myron R. Chartier. *Preaching as Communication: An Interpersonal Perspective.* Abingdon Preaching Library. William D. Thompson, ed. Nashville: Abingdon Press, 1981.

Joan D. Chittister. *Wisdom Distilled from the Daily: Living the Rule of St. Benedict Today.* San Francisco: HarperSanFrancisco, 1990.

Constitution of the World Health Organization (July 22, 1946), as found online at www.yale.edu/lawweb/avalon/decade/decad051.htm.

Phil Cousineau. *The Art of Pilgrimage: The Seeker's Guide to Making Travel Sacred.* Berkeley, Calif.: Conari Press, 1998.

Joseph Dispenza. *The Way of the Traveler: Making Every Trip a Journey of Self-Discovery.* Santa Fe, N.M.: John Muir Publications, 1999.

Doris Donnelly. *Spiritual Fitness: Everyday Exercises for Body and Soul.* San Francisco: HarperSanFrancisco, 1993.

Tilden Edwards. *Sabbath Time*. Nashville: Upper Room Books, 1992.

Vernard Eller. *The Simple Life: The Christian Stance toward Possessions*. Grand Rapids: William B. Eerdmans Publishing Company, 1973.

Clyde E. Fant. *Preaching for Today*. New York: Harper & Row Publishers, 1975.

Richard J. Foster. *Celebration of Discipline: The Path to Spiritual Growth*, rev. ed. San Francisco: HarperSanFrancisco, 1988.

Andy Gaus, trans. *The Unvarnished Gospels*. Threshold Books, 1988.

Jack Gilbert. *Monolithus: Poems, 1962 and 1982*.

Edward Hays. *Prayers for the Domestic Church: A Handbook for Worship in the Home*. Leavenworth, Kans.: Forest of Peace Publishing, 1979.

————. *Prayers for a Planetary Pilgrim: A Personal Manual for Prayer and Ritual*. Easton, Kans.: Forest of Peace Books, Inc., 1989.

Marty Haugen. "Evening Prayer," in *Holden Evening Prayer*. Copyright © 1990 GIA.

————. "Healer of Our Every Ill," in *Hymnal: A Worship Book*. Elgin, Ill.: Brethren Press; Newton, Kans.: Faith and Life Press; and Scottdale, Pa.: Mennonite Publishing House, 1992.

Barry Leisch. *The New Worship: Straight Talk on Music and the Church*. Grand Rapids: Baker Books, 1996.

Martin Luther. "Foreword," in *Symphoniae*. Georg Rhau, ed. 1538. Quoted online in Charles K. Moss.

Ken Medema. "The Gathering." Copyright © 1977 Word Music (A division of Word, Inc.). Reprinted by permission of the author.

Dara Molloy. "Creative Worship in the Celtic Tradition," in *Celtic Threads*. Padraigín Clancy, ed. Dublin: Veritas Publications, 1999.

Thomas Moore. *Care of the Soul: How to Add Depth and Meaning to Your Everyday Life*. New York: HarperCollins, 1998.

Charles K. Moss. "The Musical Reforms of Luther." Online www.composers.net/general/articles/Luther.

David Ng and Virginia Thomas. *Children in the Worshiping Community*. Atlanta: John Knox Press, 1981.

Henri J. M. Nouwen. *The Inner Voice of Love: A Journey through*

Anguish to Freedom. New York: Doubleday, 1996.

Peter M. Senge with Margaret Wheatley. "Changing How We Work Together." *Shambhala Sun.* (January 2001): 29-33.

———. *The Fifth Discipline: The Art and Practice of the Learning Organization.* New York: Currency Doubleday, 1990.

John E. Skoglund. *Worship in the Free Churches.* Valley Forge, Pa.: Judson Press, 1965.

Seventh-day Adventists Believe …: A Biblical Exposition of 27 Fundamental Doctrines. Washington, D.C.: Ministerial Association, General Conference of Seventh-day Adventists, 1988.

Songs and Prayers from Taizé. Chicago: GIA Publications, Inc., 1991.

Trust on Earth: Taizé. Ateliers et Presses de Taizé, 1998.

John Michael Talbot. "Send Us Out." Birdwing Music/Cherry Lane Music Publishing Co., Inc., 1984. Administrated by EMI Christian Music Publishing. International copyright secured. All rights reserved. Used by permission.

Evelyn Underhill. *Worship.* New York: Harper & Brothers Publishers, 1936.

Jane E. Vennard. *Praying with Body and Soul: A Way to Intimacy with God.* Minneapolis: Augsburg Fortress Publishers, 1998.

James F. White. *Introduction to Christian Worship.* Nashville: Abingdon Press, 1980.

Macrina Wiederkehr. *Behold Your Life: A Pilgrimage through Your Memories.* Notre Dame: Ave Maria Press, Inc., 2000.

Wendy M. Wright. *Sacred Dwelling: A Spirituality of Family Life.* New York: The Crossroad Publishing Company, 1989.